Advance Praise for *Race Crazy*

"Most of us think we understand Black Lives Matter. We don't. Charles Love has delved into Black Lives Matter and found there is much more to the group and the movement than almost any of us know. For the people BLM ostensibly serves, Love has a warning: 'It is likely they do not know the extent to which Black Lives Matter is fighting against their interests.' This is one of the most important books at this perilous moment in American history."

—Dennis Prager, Nationally Syndicated Radio Show Host, President of PragerU, and *New York Times* Bestselling Author of Several Books, Most Recently Volume Three of *The Rational Bible*

"Charles Love's new book *Race Crazy* is a must-read to understand how truly dangerous the BLM movement and The 1619 Project are to the future of this country. Instead of offering solutions, BLM foments the fear and resentment that only exacerbate the problems facing everyday black Americans. Mr. Love offers us all a way to fight back."

—Bob Woodson, President of The Woodson Center and Founder of 1776 Unites

"Who is Black Lives Matter actually helping? What is the real impact on black Americans of The 1619 Project? Charles Love's *Race Crazy* takes a deep dive into the philosophy, funding, and objectives of BLM and the impact on people of color of the thoroughly fraudulent 1619 Project. It could not come at a better time. African Americans across the nation need to squelch these anti-black and anti-American initiatives while they still have the freedom to do so."

—Larry Schweikart, Professor of History, Co-author, *A Patriot's History of the United States*

"Race craziness is a problem affecting too many Americans and this book is long overdue in the discussion of racism in America. Where is that 'honest conversation' so many people claim to want to have? What we get instead is media-sponsored narratives followed by proclamations of racism on everything. Hard work, math, God, and black holes are but a few of the things deemed racist by the propagandists and other accusers. In Love's book, he provides the road map to start the conversation we should be having. *Race Crazy* explores the perpetual cycle of name calling and misinformation and puts into context the BLM movement and the 1619 Project from a truthful perspective."

—Kevin Jackson, Host, *The Kevin Jackson Show*, Founder of The Black Sphere

"Charles Love separates rhetoric from reality in his new book, *Race Crazy,* where he addresses Black Lives Matter, The 1619 Project, and the new progressive racism movement. The book is deeply researched and eloquently makes the case for American principles. As our nation is consumed by racial politics, Love offers clarity, insight, and commitment to policies that would make the country better—not drag it backward."

—Chris Rufo, Senior Fellow and Director of the initiative on critical race theory at the Manhattan Institute, and Founder of Battlefront—a center for narrative, legal, and policy warfare

"With his new book *Race Crazy*, Charles Love takes his place among a new wave of Black thinkers questioning the tactics, logic, and conclusions, of today's 'woke' movement. The book opens by asking a very simple and important question: when exactly—at least in the modern era—did Americans become absolutely obsessed with emphasizing racial differences? Further, why would any of us expect the things he discusses, such as sorting schoolchildren by race or arguing about the exact percentage of minority superheroes in comic books, will produce a better and less conflicted society? No one could agree with every one of any author's conclusions, but Love makes a very solid case that America would be better served by a return to trying our best for color blindness than by today's guilty, obsessive racial bean counting. Read his book, and listen to our podcast!"

—Wilfred Reilly, Professor of Political Science at Kentucky State University, Author of *Hate Crime Hoax* and *Taboo*, Co-Host, *Cut The Bull Podcast* with Charles Love and Shemeka Michelle

"Charles Love has written a beautiful and highly stylized work that can truly be described as death by impeccable logic and reason to BLM and The 1619 Project. This book is a brilliant tour de force that identifies and then destroys with surgical precision the false claims made by both movements. More importantly, Charles Love has exposed the egregious harm they inflict on the moral reputation of all black Americans—the nefarious indictment they make against America as an evil country. Love sets the record straight in debunking these shibboleths and, in the process, restores grandeur and honor to America, and reminds us of the promise of hope, redemption, and prosperity she delivers to those blessed to live up to her name."

—Jason D. Hill, Professor of Philosophy, DePaul University, Author of *What Do White Americans Owe Black People?: Racial Justice in the Age of Post-Oppression*

RACE CRAZY

BLM, 1619, AND THE PROGRESSIVE RACISM MOVEMENT

CHARLES LOVE

EMANCIPATION BOOKS

AN EMPANCIPATION BOOKS BOOK
An Imprint of Post Hill Press
ISBN: 978-1-64293-841-8
ISBN (eBook): 978-1-64293-842-5

Race Crazy:
BLM, 1619, and the Progressive Racism Movement

Cover Design by Tiffani Shea

Post Hill Press
New York • Nashville
posthillpress.com

Published in the United States of America
1 2 3 4 5 6 7 8 9 10

To the youth being harmed and led astray by the progressive racism movement. I hope this can serve as a tool to overcome the heightened focus on immutable traits and encourage free thinking.

Contents

Introduction

Our country has gone race crazy. Race has become an obsession, and those pushing this madness are leading the country into division and decline. It is important to take a nuanced approach when addressing society's biggest problems; however, our shift to an all-encompassing race focus has propelled our national conversations outside the realm of rational thinking.

We must stop pretending that this lunacy is moral, fair, legal, or helpful to blacks.

Much of this focus on race is being infiltrated into the culture through our education system. From K-12 schools, where our impressionable children spend their formative years, to the hallowed halls of our institutions of higher learning, administrators have decided that blacks are different from others and therefore should be treated differently. The negative impact of years of lowering standards, affirmative action admissions, and racially biased grade manipulations have harmed the education of blacks, their likelihood of graduation, and their prospects for post-college success. These race-conscious biases also set a precedent for today's far more radical race-based discrimination.

At UCLA, a professor was suspended for refusing to cancel final exams for black students after George Floyd was killed.[1] The University of Chicago showed its allegiance to the cause by mandating all applicants for graduate-level English programs work in "Black Studies."[2] At some institutions, the once-unthinkable is occurring, as racially segregated clubs, graduations, and dormitories have returned. What is happening in K-12 schools may be more shocking. A biracial high school student in a Nevada charter school was challenged to identify as "privileged" or "oppressed" in a racial identity test.[3] A California elementary school forced third-graders to deconstruct their racial identities.[4]

The 1960s Civil Rights movement, championed by Dr. Martin Luther King and other courageous advocates of racial equality, has been stood on its head. In our now race-obsessed society, one's identity—long regarded as personal and self-created—has reverted to being tribal and genetically determined.

---

1 Natalie O'Neill, "UCLA professor suspended after refusing leniency for black students," *New York Post,* June 10, 2020. https://nypost.com/2020/06/10/ucla-suspends-professor-for-refusing-leniency-for-black-students/

2 Bradford Betz, "UChicago English department: Grad applicants accepted only for work 'in and with Black Studies,'" FoxNews.com (online), September 14, 2020. https://www.foxnews.com/us/university-chicago-english-department-grad-applicants-accepted-only-black-studies

3 Alex Swoyer, "Nevada student sues charter school over social justice curriculum," *The Washington Times,* March 21, 2021. https://www.washingtontimes.com/news/2021/mar/21/nevada-student-sues-charter-school-over-social-jus/

4 Christopher F. Rufo, "Woke elementary," *City Journal,* January 13, 2021. https://www.city-journal.org/identity-politics-in-cupertino-california-elementary-school

How race crazy have things become? There was the judge who ruled a black defendant could not get a fair trial because there were portraits of white judges in the courtroom[5]; the CEO of Chick-fil-A who said whites should shine the shoes of black strangers[6]; and a study from Ohio State University that suggested victims of racism should take psychedelic drugs to lessen their "trauma"[7]; an article in *Psychology Today* that argued "racial microaggressions" cause PTSD.[8] Consider also the argument by Brandon Hasbrouck, assistant professor at Washington and Lee University School of Law. At a time when many were contesting the fairness of election results, and "social justice warriors" were demanding we "count all the votes," Professor Hasbrouck decided to go in a different

5 Justin Jouvenal, "Va. Judge rules Black defendant can't get a fair trial in courtroom largely featuring portraits of White judges," *The Washington Post*, December 22, 2020. https://www.washingtonpost.com/local/legal-issues/courtroom-portraits-judges-ruling/2020/12/22/366c57a8-445e-11eb-975c-d17b8815a66d_story.html

6 Keith Griffith, "Chick-fil-A CEO makes bizarre plea for white people to repent for racism by 'shining a black stranger's shoes,'" *Daily Mail Online*, June 20, 2020. https://www.dailymail.co.uk/news/article-8443159/Chick-fil-CEO-urges-white-people-repent-racism-shining-black-strangers-shoes.html

7 Emily Caldwell, "One psychedelic experience may lessen trauma of racial injustice," *Ohio State News*, December 28, 2020. https://news.osu.edu/one-psychedelic-experience-may-lessen-trauma-of-racial-injustice/

8 Monnica T. Williams, Ph.D., "The link between racism and PTSD," *Psychology Today*, September 6, 2015. https://www.psychologytoday.com/us/blog/culturally-speaking/201509/the-link-between-racism-and-ptsd

direction. He posits that we need to implement "vote reparations," by counting the votes of black Americans twice.[9]

Any serious person can see how these things are the opposite of equality, will magnify social hostility, and will do more harm than good. These foolish demands increase in proportion to the ground we cede by giving in to them, or simply by pretending such demands or actions are reasonable and to be taken seriously. Our silent acquiescence in the face of the irrational and immoral is only bolstering these activists, which is leading to a societal breakdown. That can no longer be tolerated. Borrowing from the radicals themselves, we must "resist."

This is what *Race Crazy* sets out to do. It is about what I call "the progressive racism movement"—an extreme left-wing movement organized to re-engineer society by judging and treating people according to their skin color. Ironically, this is done under the guise of rooting out racism. Adherents to this movement use race as the primary factor in many decisions, but they don't believe it is racist to do so because of their intent. No matter how well-intentioned they are, their actions display their contempt for whites and a condescending view of blacks. The book will describe, in great detail, why this movement is dangerous, and what we need to do to reverse the racist trend they are promoting.

"We are five days away from fundamentally transforming the United States of America." This famous line was proclaimed by Barack Obama, then a candidate for president, at a rally in Columbia, Missouri, just days before the 2008 presidential

---

9 Brandon Hasbrouck, "The votes of Black Americans should count twice," *The Nation*, December 17, 2020. https://www.thenation.com/article/society/black-votes-reparations-gerrymandering/

election.[10] No one could have guessed that the transformation he never achieved would be ushered in by a man dying in police custody in Minneapolis.

The video of George Floyd on the ground, pinned under an officer's knee, and his subsequent death, led to mass protests and calls for change. But what change? This emotionally charged incident has created an environment where critical thinking is discouraged, if not abandoned. It is being used to indict all police officers and the entire country. Otherwise, reasonable people have been convinced that we are back in 1950s Selma: all police officers are Bull Connor, all criminal suspects are innocent victims of racial oppression and police aggression, and all of American society is "systemically racist" and requires radical change.

The spearhead of this crusade is the organization known as Black Lives Matter. Consider only two among the many problems caused by their "social justice" approach.

The first is exaggerating the issue of police brutality. This is the entire basis of Black Lives Matter's existence. They are convinced that there is a systematic plot by police to exterminate blacks, that it is born out of racism, and that it is approved by government leaders. Sensible people know this is not true, but it seems we are finding fewer sensible people every day.

Anyone seeking to determine if their argument has merit need only look at the statistics. The number of police shootings is relatively small compared to the population of the country and the number of violent crimes that are committed each year. When

---

10 David Weigel, "Fundamentally transforming the United States of America," *Slate*, October 18, 2011. https://slate.com/news-and-politics/2011/10/fundamentally-transforming-the-united-states-of-america.html

addressing police shootings and racial concerns, conservatives often fall into the trap of comparing this number to the number of violent crimes committed against blacks by other blacks. This is an unwinnable argument and totally unnecessary. Those arguing that blacks are subject to an onslaught of state-sanctioned violence don't need to be told that blacks commit crime too, they need to see the truth of police shootings in context.

In the six-year period from January 1, 2015 through December 31, 2020, there were 5,949 people killed by police, 1,396 of them black men, according to the *Washington Post*, which has meticulously tracked this data in their police shooting database.[11] Immediately we see that black men represent only 25 percent of the total number of police killings. To further disprove their argument, one could contrast the police shooting data with the FBI's violent crime data.

There were at least seven hundred thousand violent crimes committed in 2019. It is safe to assume that some of these criminals resisted arrest or attacked the arresting officer. If 1 percent of them were killed by police, that would be seven times the actual number of people killed by police that year.

But the claim is that there is a racial factor that exponentially increases the rate of police shooting for blacks. Let us examine the violent crime statistics among blacks.[12] It is universally understood that most criminals and victims are of the same race,

---

[11] Julie Tate, Jennifer Jenkins, and Steven Rich, "946 people have been shot and killed by police in the past year," *Washington Post*, Updated June 3, 2021. https://www.washingtonpost.com/graphics/investigations/police-shootings-database/

[12] Federal Bureau of Investigation, "Table 43: Arrests by Race and Ethnicity," 2019. https://ucr.fbi.gov/crime-in-the-u.s/2019/crime-in-the-u.s.-2019/topic-pages/tables/table-43

therefore we can assume in most cases that if the person committing the crime is black, the victim is likely black. Here are the number of blacks arrested by violent crime category in 2019: Murder—4,078, Rape—4,427, Robbery—29,677, Aggravated Assault—91,164. In this one year alone, there were three times as many blacks raped, twenty-one times as many robbed, and sixty-five times as many violently assaulted as there were blacks killed by police in the six years reported combined.

Whatever improvements are needed, the argument that the police are hunting down black men is unsubstantiated and can be easily disproven with an honest analysis of the facts. Even the *Washington Post*, who created their police shooting database to highlight the problem, wrote in May of 2018 that fatal police shootings of unarmed people have significantly declined.[13] The numbers have held constant in the three years since the article was written.

You can give people mountains of such statistics, but facts no longer seem to matter in the face of the toxic, "racist cop" narrative.

A second problem with this "cop bad, suspect good" bias is that it ignores, excuses, or condones bad, often criminal, behavior by some black suspects when interacting with police to prove racism is pervasive.

While the intent may be to help someone assumed to have been wronged by police, elevating people who, at minimum,

---

[13] John Sullivan, Julie Tate, and Jennifer Jenkins, "Fatal police shootings of unarmed people have significantly declined, experts say," May 8, 2018. https://www.washingtonpost.com/investigations/fatal-police-shootings-of-unarmed-people-have-significantly-declined-experts-say/2018/05/03/d5eab374-4349-11e8-8569-26fda6b404c7_story.html

made bad decisions and, in most cases, committed violent crimes, to martyrs or donating large sums of money to them will lead to more violent interactions with police in the future as suspects become more emboldened to be aggressive toward police.

Rayshard Brooks was shot and killed by police in Atlanta on June 12, 2020. The police were called because Brooks had fallen asleep in his car, which was blocking a Wendy's drive-through lane. The incident was captured on video. The video shows him fail a field sobriety test, fight with officers, steal a taser, and fire it at an officer who was chasing him.[14] In response to his death, there were riots and protests around the country and the Wendy's where he slept in his car was burned to the ground. In addition to this lawlessness, a GoFundMe page supporting him has raised over $265,000.[15]

Another example of being rewarded for bad behavior is Jacob Blake. Blake was shot in Kenosha, Wisconsin in August of 2020 after resisting arrest during a domestic dispute. The officers responded to a call and found he had an outstanding warrant for sexual assault. Again, protests and riots followed. A church, along with several businesses, were set ablaze. Blake's defenders claimed he was unarmed although he admitted in an interview on *Good Morning America* that he had a knife in his

---

14 Malachy Browne, Christina Kelso, and Barbara Marcolini, "How Rayshard Brooks was fatally shot by the Atlanta police," *The New York Times*, June 14, 2020. https://www.nytimes.com/2020/06/14/us/videos-rayshard-brooks-shooting-atlanta-police.html

15 Stewart Trial Attorneys, "Official GoFundMe for Rayshard Brooks," GoFundMe, June 13, 2020. https://gofund.me/45f699d2

hand at the time.[16] Despite the facts in the case, his GoFundMe page raised over $600,000 in one day and the current tally is nearly $2.4 million.[17] [18]

Then there is the unfortunate termination of Officer Michael Oxford. Oxford was a police officer in Gwinnett, Georgia. He responded to a complaint where a woman said her neighbor threatened to murder her. She showed the officer a video of the altercation, and he went to the home to investigate and found three women sitting on a porch, one of whom he recognized from the video. He asked the woman to come talk to him, and she refused, while the other women continued to interject.

He then told everyone to shut up, except the woman he needed to interview. That was when Kyndesia Smith got loud and argumentative. She told the officer she did not have to comply. He asked her if she wanted to go to jail, to which she replied, "I'm not going to jail." He told her she was obstructing his investigation and would be arrested if she did not move. She refused, saying, "I'm not resisting but don't touch me." After she made repeated attempts to evade him, he tased her. He called for backup and after getting her to the police car, she lunged at him

---

16 Brittany De Lea, "Jacob Blake admits he had a knife when he was shot by police," *Fox News*, January 14, 2021. https://www.foxnews.com/us/jacob-blake-knife-shot-police

17 Khaleda Rahman, "Jacob Blake GoFundMe raises more than $650K in less than a day," *Newsweek*, August 25, 2020. https://www.newsweek.com/gofundme-jacob-blake-surpasses-650k-1527380

18 Julia Jackson, "Justice for Jacob Blake," GoFundMe, August 24, 2020. https://gofund.me/e50dd071

when he tried to put her in the car. The entire scene was captured on his body cam video.[19]

The department conducted a three-pronged investigation. On the arrest, they said he was within policy to arrest her. On the use of force, they determined that it was appropriate based on her actions, but then concluded that he had not been courteous enough. "One of our core values is courtesy. We strive to conduct ourselves in a manner that promotes mutual respect with the community and our peers."[20] Finally, you can hear the woman filming Officer Oxford saying, "You're going to get sued." Obviously, she had seen how these incidents have played out in recent years.

Black Lives Matter has fomented contempt for police officers and a widespread view of all blacks as innocent victims. If the reduction of proactive policing is a result of the "Ferguson Effect," then punishing officers and celebrating criminals is the "Black Lives Matter Effect." This effect is far more widespread and dangerous.

Black Lives Matter tells whites that blacks are not only terrorized victims of cops but also victims of "systemic racism" and "white privilege," and thereby need to be swaddled in the comforts generated from white guilt, including racial reparations.

---

19 General General, "Officer M. Oxford terminated after viral video of Kyndesia Smith's arrest, Gwinnett PD, Georgia, USA," August 22, 2020. Posted on YouTube at https://www.youtube.com/watch?v=Z-byZDAzXKI

20 Minyvonne Burke, "Georgia officer fired after video shows him using stun gun on woman during arrest," *NBC News*, August 22, 2020. https://www.nbcnews.com/news/us-news/georgia-officer-fired-after-video-shows-him-using-stun-gun-n1237773

Black Lives Matter also is infecting the black community. Prior to the death of George Floyd, the group was largely ignored among blacks. I now see many blacks wearing Black Lives Matter T-shirts and using the hashtag.

Black Lives Matter's founding principle and claims are wrong, as the data clearly show. The facts are readily available and have been written about frequently enough that ignorance is not a valid excuse. I will further show that Black Lives Matter is not focused on the needs of the black community. You will find no solutions or rational demands from them. This is not an error of omission.

As I dug deeper into the movement, I found that Black Lives Matter is not designed to effect any real change. They are primarily the chaos arm of a larger apparatus. When the police shoot someone, it is BLM's job to get people to the scene and to protest. Protestors start looting? It is Black Lives Matter who comes out and says, "Looting is reparations." They can be heard saying, "If we don't get what we want, we will burn the country to the ground," but they never clearly say exactly what it is that they want.

This is being done to give cover to a well-organized, well-funded, powerful force within the Black Lives Matter movement—a group it is likely most Americans have never heard of. The organization is the Movement for Black Lives. In a kind of ventriloquist/dummy relationship, the Movement for Black Lives is Jeff Dunham and Black Lives Matter is Peanut.[21]

Here is how the Movement for Black Lives describes itself:

---

[21] Jeff Dunham website: https://www.jeffdunham.com/character/walter/peanut/

> The Movement for Black Lives (M4BL) is an ecosystem of individuals and organizations creating a shared vision and policy agenda to win rights, recognition, and resources for Black people. In doing so, the movement makes it possible for us, and therefore everyone, to live healthy and fruitful lives. While Black Lives Matter gets all the press, the Movement for Black Lives coordinates this collection of groups, each with a unique and specific focus within the growing network. Some focus on issues like income inequality, school discipline, and abortion. Others address various so-called "intersectional" groups, like LGBTQ, DACA, and incarcerated people. Still others work on policy initiatives and political influence.

All this activity is coordinated by a shadowy organization that only pops up on the periphery. You Google them and get few hits. They do not send representatives out to do interviews, and you rarely hear from them. But you hear their voice and feel their presence in every other group they support.

Here is an example of a time they indirectly got media coverage. On September 3, 2020, in a *Tucker Carlson Tonight* investigative segment, host Carlson discussed alleged direct ties between Democrats and the urban riots.[22] He mentioned an

[22] Tucker Carlson, *Tucker Carlson Tonight*, Fox News, September 3, 2020. Episode segment archived at: https://archive.org/details/FOXNEWSW_20200904_000000_Tucker_Carlson_Tonight/start/1740/end/1800

organization, the Black Visions Collective, and claimed to have found evidence that the group organized the Minneapolis riots. He put up an image of what most would assume was their logo, but it did not say Black Visions Collective; it said: In Defense of Black Life. Above it was the logo for Movement for Black Lives. Yet, there was no mention of the master group.

Unlike these other groups, which either have no websites or have nearly empty pages with meaningless feel-good phrases, the Movement for Black Lives website has detailed information stating who they are, what they believe, and their clear vision for America. They have a platform that reads like a constitution, complete with a preamble. They have a list of demands with proposed legislation to back it up. Lest you think they are all bark, they have an entire fund dedicated to supporting their dangerous platform—and unwitting corporations are lining up to fill their coffers.

The last part of this progressive racism movement is The 1619 Project. This is the project launched by the *New York Times Magazine* to give, in their eyes, a true depiction of the history of America. While this project is not directly tied to Black Lives Matter, it, too, is hyper-focused on race and based on half-truths and false syllogisms. The author, Nikole Hannah-Jones, and her acolytes argue that America was founded on slavery and racism, and those tenets permeate the entirety of the country's past as well as the racial discrepancies we see today.[23]

The project is racist on its face. It purports that all whites are racist, going down the same line of reasoning as the anti-black

---

[23] Nikole Hannah-Jones et al., "The 1619 Project," *New York Times Magazine*, August 14, 2019. https://www.nytimes.com/interactive/2019/08/14/magazine/1619-america-slavery.html

racists it claims to decry. It is also anti-American, politically skewed, and, like all race-led movements, supportive of inequality that benefits its preferred group. What is most dangerous is its level of support. Just as corporations and politicians are working to advance Black Lives Matter's demands, left-leaning academics, teachers unions, and school administrators are adding this historically revisionist misinformation to school curriculums across the country.

Critical race theory is a term we are hearing a lot today so I want to explain why there is little direct mention of it in the book. When I started this quest, my goal was to give people a clear understanding of what is happening in our culture and how damaging it is. In doing research for the book, I found that there were various people and groups doing the same destructive work under different names. Today we hear critical race theory along with white fragility, anti-racist, and critical social justice. I focus on The 1619 Project because it ushered in the others and is the one that is most predominately influencing the curricula being added to our public schools.

This is also why I use the term *progressive racism* because all these demands, and any new ones, like *equity over equality*, are just new ways of saying the same thing. Discrimination, or more accurately, racism, is encouraged if advanced by the right people for the right reasons. No organization more clearly expresses the beliefs of the progressive racism movement than The 1619 Project.

Race Crazy will show how this movement, under the guise of addressing "systemic racism," actually sets back race relations and undermines the values of our nation. Black Lives Matter generates anger and fear while making enemies of police and most whites; the Movement for Black Lives spreads disinformation and proposes legislation that promotes inequality; and The 1619 Project presents racialized fiction as American history, aimed at shaming and dispiriting whites, while making blacks feel like entitled victims.

These three toxic organizations constitute a brilliantly convoluted, anti-American coalition of activists, journalists, financiers, politicians, entertainers, and others pushing for what they call "restorative justice," a goal that is an anathema to actual justice. They also perpetuate an intentionally false narrative, alleging that racism is the reason for every disparity in America. Critical race theory, "systemic racism," and all other elements of their poorly crafted arguments are the foundation on which the progressive racism movement is built.

It is important for me to state that this is not a political book. In fact, much of my communication here is directed to blacks, independents, and left-leaning individuals who sincerely want to see improvements in the country at large and the black community specifically, but who unintentionally are contributing to our problems by supporting this movement. To these readers I wish to address some initial questions:

Black Lives Matter has gone from widely dismissed fringe radicals to mainstream status; but are they a force for good? The Movement for Black Lives is a conduit for many black-led organizations; but if they are striving for equality, why the secrecy? The 1619 Project looks to re-educate America about its ugly, divisive history, showing that blacks are largely locked out of the liberty and pursuit of happiness it promises; but can America fairly be boiled down only or even primarily to racism?

Race Crazy will answer these questions. Liberals, blacks, and independent people of goodwill need to know the truth. No matter how good their intentions, they cannot fix any of our divisive social issues by working with people who are hostile toward America's founding principles and hellbent on destroying them. Once readers see these groups' beliefs described in their own words, there will be little doubt that this movement is not about police brutality or treating everyone equally. What they really want is special treatment for some at the expense of others. All their essays, arguments, and rhetoric point to past injustices, but their proposed remedies seek to re-create a system of inequalities, merely inverting the beneficiaries and victims.

My goal is to offer fair-minded readers a logical analysis of these groups' beliefs and demands. I will show how they are un-American, unenforceable, and suppress equality rather than support it. You will be shocked to know that any supposedly credible organization would be willing to post these demands on its website, or that any politician or corporation would take these ideas and demands seriously. Unfortunately, they *are* being taken seriously, and if these demands are accepted, our beloved country *will* be fundamentally transformed, but in ways the overwhelming majority of us—of whatever race—will find horrifying and repugnant.

Finally, it is important to note that I took all the quotes, demands, and actions listed in the book directly from the Black Lives Matter and Movement for Black Lives websites as well as essays within The 1619 Project. As the movement drew more attention and many well-deserved attacks, they started to make adjustments to their sites, often removing information that would seem controversial. For instance, the often-cited language about the nuclear family is gone from the Black Lives Matter website. I can only assume that as they get more scrutiny, and after the book is released, there will be more changed. The information is accurate as of the time of the writing.

BLM

1

A False Premise

"Black people are being slaughtered in the streets, killed in their homes." This is the tearful plea from actress Julianne Moore, in a cringe-worthy video from an assortment of celebrities vowing, "I take responsibility."[24] While any reasonable person should find that line impossible to take seriously, it is the premise for which Black Lives Matter is based. Here is how the group's website describes its formation.

Black Lives Matter was founded in 2013 by three self-described "radical Black organizers"—Alicia Garza, Patrisse Cullors, and Opal Tometi. The movement was created in response to the acquittal of George Zimmerman for the murder of Trayvon Martin. Black Lives Matter is, as Garza states, "a

[24] Julianne Moore et al., "I take responsibility," Public Service Announcement, On Demand Entertainment, June 11, 2020. Posted on YouTube at https://www.youtube.com/watch?v=YdsmxzaHtSQ

globally recognized organizing project that focuses on combating anti-Black state-sanctioned violence and the oppression of all Black people."

Right from the beginning, there is a factual challenge to their account of the George Zimmerman case. This was a highly scrutinized case, and varying opinions are understandable. Some believe Zimmerman's account and think he acted in self-defense. Others think he was overzealous and should not have put Trayvon in that situation. Both are reasonable assessments and, without video evidence, the verdict could have gone either way. What is not in question is that describing this case as "state-sanctioned violence" is shockingly dishonest.

The verdict was not state-sanctioned; a jury of citizens found him not guilty. George Zimmerman was not a member of "the state" as he was not acting on behalf of the government. And where was the proof of any anti-black sentiment? Not one piece of evidence was presented suggesting that Zimmerman was using race as a factor in his actions. In fact, *NBC News* was caught editing the tape of Zimmerman's 911 call to make it seem as if he followed Martin because he was black; they later issued an apology and fired the producer.[25] Yet, Black Lives Matter was formed to correct this invented problem.

This could be forgiven if it had been a one-time error in judgment—if they had gotten too far ahead of themselves and later realized the error of their ways. But this would soon become their modus operandi: ride into town, attack everything as racist,

---

[25] Wendy Carpenter, "NBC fires producer over edited Zimmerman 911 call," *Yahoo! News*, April 7, 2012. https://www.yahoo.com/news/blogs/upshot/nbc-fires-producer-over-edited-zimmerman-911-call-201124740.html

claim there was a miscarriage of justice, kindle a fire within the community, then leave. The website continues, "A year later, we set out together on the Black Lives Matter Freedom Ride to Ferguson, in search of justice for Mike Brown…."

How can they be seeking justice for Michael Brown? Unlike the Zimmerman case, we have a clearer picture of what happened here. There is no video of the altercation, but there were several eyewitness accounts of the actual shooting, with some witnesses claiming to see a struggle, while others testified only to seeing the chase. Most of the witnesses confirmed Officer Darren Wilson's account of the shooting, almost universally stating that Michael Brown never had his hands up or said, "Don't shoot!" The few witnesses whose stories aligned with the account by Dorian Johnson,[26] Michael Brown's friend and companion at the time of the shooting, either recanted or admitted that they were friends of Brown, Johnson, or both.

Most compelling was the grand jury testimony of Ciara Jenkins, one member of a family of five who witnessed the shooting from a nearby minivan.[27] She testified that Michael Brown closed his hand like a fist and ran toward the officer; Wilson backed away; and she heard him repeatedly yell, "Stop!"

---

[26] Robert Siegel, interview with Freeman Bosley, "An account of the Ferguson shooting, from the man standing beside Brown," *All Things Considered*, National Public Radio, August 18, 2014. https://www.npr.org/2014/08/18/341426635/an-account-of-the-ferguson-shooting-from-the-man-standing-beside-brown

[27] Kevin Mooney, "Using grand jury testimony, 'Ferguson' stage play challenges media narratives," *The Daily Signal*, November 9, 2017. https://www.dailysignal.com/2017/11/09/using-grand-jury-testimony-ferguson-stage-play-challenges-media-narratives/

Jenkins stated, "He was running toward him like a football tackle, like he was going to tackle the officer. If he got close enough, I feel like he would have tackled him against the car.... I am not, you know, really big on talking to the police or defending the police, or anything like that. I am just being real [sic] honest with you. I feel like the officer, was in the right. And that is a lot of saying, because other than that, I ain't got nothing to do with them." Even Eric Holder, Attorney General under Barack Obama, found there was not enough evidence to indict Darren Wilson.[28]

If Black Lives Matter truly had been "in search of justice for Mike Brown," they should have been searching through the grand jury transcripts. It is from this fabricated case of police murder that they were able to create a national movement. In 2020, many people were still counting Michael Brown among unarmed black men wrongfully killed by the police. They were still marking the anniversary of his death as if he were shot on a balcony in Memphis in 1968.

Black Lives Matter uses the same method when addressing any high-profile case involving police and blacks: draw the most outlandish assumptions from few to no facts, then amplify the rhetoric. Let us look at another example: the death of Breonna Taylor.

Taylor, a twenty-six-year-old black woman, was shot and killed by Louisville Metro Police Department (LMPD) in a

28 Memorandum, "Department of Justice report regarding the criminal investigation into the shooting death of Michael Brown by Ferguson, Missouri Police Officer Darren Wilson," U.S. Department of Justice, March 4, 2015. https://www.justice.gov/sites/default/files/opa/press-releases/attachments/2015/03/04/doj_report_on_shooting_of_michael_brown_1.pdf

raid on March 13, 2020. We know that Taylor was suspected of dealing drugs, there was a warrant to search her home, she was approaching the door when the police entered, her boyfriend fired first, and then Taylor was struck eight times in the ensuing gunfire.[29] The case is, as of this writing, under investigation, and two of the three officers involved have been placed on administrative assignment, while the third has been terminated.

This means nothing in relation to Taylor's guilt or innocence. But as is the case with many of these incidents, the public only has partial information. This lack of information is where people with an agenda are prone to invent things. Activists claim that either the police entered the wrong house *or* they had the person they were looking for in custody, so there was no reason to enter her home. Extremists disguised as journalists argue she was asleep in her bed when she was killed.[30] The evidence does not support any of these arguments, but sadly, once false information is fed to the public, it is difficult to refute. (Remember, "Hands Up, Don't Shoot!")

As a result of this propaganda barrage, everyone from Beyoncé to LeBron James demanded justice for Breonna. Oprah made her the only person besides herself—narcissism knows no

---

29 Tessa Duvall, "FACT CHECK 2.0: Separating the truth from the lies in the Breonna Taylor police shooting," *Louisville Courier Journal*, June 16, 2020; updated March 17, 2021. https://www.azcentral.com/story/news/crime/2020/06/16/breonna-taylor-fact-check-7-rumors-wrong/5326938002/

30 Marquis Francis, "'Sleeping while black': Family seeks justice for Breonna Taylor, killed in her bedroom by police," *Yahoo! News*, May 13, 2020. https://news.yahoo.com/asleep-while-black-family-seeks-justice-for-breonna-taylor-killed-in-her-bedroom-by-police-210858395.html

bounds—ever to grace the cover of *O* magazine. Countless Black Lives Matter supporters mention her case as evidence of police murdering innocent blacks.

Those who disagree with Black Lives Matter or who are bothered by the negative perception of police officers understand how bad this is. Those who champion Black Lives Matter's cause are also affected by their incorrect assumptions. If they are wrong about the cause of the problem, how can they offer adequate solutions to solve it?

DeRay McKesson is an activist and member of Campaign Zero. Campaign Zero was formed in 2015 by a group of activists and researchers to collect and publicize police department data and practices to understand how to significantly reduce police violence. A 2020 *GQ* article about McKesson's work explains, "The research that led to #8Can'tWait also began in 2015 with what soon became the Police Use of Force Project—a numbers-driven, reader-friendly examination of the violent tactics that police departments in America's 100 largest cities employ. The idea is that, if police departments adopt eight reforms of when and how they use force, the ensuing data shows a significant drop in killings—as much as 72 percent if all eight are followed. The policies are as follows:"[31]

- Ban chokeholds and strangleholds
- Require de-escalation
- Require warning before shooting

[31] Alex Schultz, "DeRay Mckesson on the 8 reforms that could dramatically reduce police violence," MSN.com, June 3, 2020. https://www.msn.com/en-us/news/opinion/deray-mckesson-on-the-8-reforms-that-could-dramatically-reduce-police-violence/ar-BB14YMfb

- Exhaust all other means before shooting
- Duty to intervene and stop excessive force by other officers
- Ban shooting at moving vehicle
- Require use-of-force continuum
- Require comprehensive reporting each time an officer uses forces or threatens to do so.

While none of these reforms are extreme, and although it is unclear what a "use-of-force continuum" is, they would do little to end the alleged "epidemic" of unarmed black men being shot, because they don't account for a suspect's behavior. Moreover, the idea that a fact-based, data-driven research project would determine that these eight reforms would reduce police violence by 72 percent is dubious at best.

Without access to the raw data used, it is impossible to refute their findings. However, it is unlikely that a large number of the millions of police interactions with blacks involve chokeholds or shooting at moving vehicles, so those reforms are not likely to move the needle much. Most agree that officers should try to de-escalate situations and give warnings before shooting, but it would be helpful to know how often this does not happen. Also, any *complete* research would provide information on how often people do not comply.

Training officers to stop other officers from using excessive force seems a wonderful thing, but like "exhausting all other means before shooting," who gets to dictate what is excessive and when all other means have been exhausted? Also, what happens when there is no other officer present, which is often the case?

While credit should be given to Campaign Zero for trying to find solutions—which is far more than Black Lives Matter has ever done—these reforms do not combat the types of interactions

Black Lives Matter and others protest. Of the three cases listed above, like most of the other high-profile cases, which would have been prevented by these reforms? None. Shockingly, Campaign Zero issued an apology for distracting attention from the abolition movement with its reform proposals. This is an example of how strengthening Black Lives Matter weakens the chances of compromise.

Black Lives Matter had been largely ignored and viewed, fittingly, as extreme. This all changed on May 25, 2020. On the evening of Memorial Day, George Floyd was shopping at Cup Foods and was accused of paying with a counterfeit twenty-dollar bill. The employees called the police. The now infamous video shows a police officer kneeling on Floyd's neck. He later died.

Overnight, the name of what had before seemed like a radical fringe group became the rallying cry for the nation. Emotional reactions flooded logic. Protests and violent outbursts in racial situations were not new, but this was different. There were protests in every major city in the country, many turning violent, and Black Lives Matter received international support.

This new attention was bolstered by the COVID-19 lockdowns. It is hard to believe that under normal circumstances people would have taken off work to march for thirty consecutive days. But it was a perfect storm: lockdown frustration, fear of the uncertain future, and an abundance of idle time. The country was swept up in a fervor over policing and nearly every police department across the country was being held to account for a killing caused by an individual officer. This created a windfall for Black Lives Matter, but was it warranted?

As with most of these hot-button political and social issues, people rely on emotion far too much. While it should not be completely dismissed, logic and facts should be the primary factors used in determining the risk level of a problem, and police brutality is no exception. Instead, emotion rules the day.

In the summer of 2020 alone, there were at least three high-profile police shootings, and they all followed the same script. A video is released, usually of a small section of the entire interaction; people are immediately outraged and assume racist intent; the media reports, "White cop, black suspect," and the protests start. In short order, rioting and looting begin. Finally, pandering politicians, clueless celebrities, and agitating activists push the narrative that the police are racist, and that this happens "every day." This has become the normal reaction, but are those advancing the anti-police narrative, right?

When confronting a problem, the logical thing to do is consider all possible causes and deal with each one, prioritizing them by importance. With police shootings, many find only one cause: the police. Falling into this short-sighted, hyper-emotional cycle does not deal with the reality of the problem. Anyone who refuses to consider the events that brought the police to the situation in the first place is being disingenuous and should be ignored.

Activists, protestors, and pundits will analyze a police shooting video and tell you everything the officer did wrong but never mention the victim's behavior. When the victim's behavior is brought up, a typical response is, "Committing a crime shouldn't cost you your life." While this is usually true, unless there is a violent crime being committed as the police arrive on scene as in the case of Ma'Khia Bryant, none of the victims of the high-profile police shootings that occurred in the summer of 2020 were shot because of their crimes.[32] They were shot because of their actions during the arrest.

This inevitably leads to a conversation on compliance. To many who believe police are bad, mentioning compliance is "blaming the victim" at least, or blatant racism at worst. This is an unusually perplexing stance to take. To illustrate its flaws, I use an example I call the robber scenario.

In this scenario, a man is walking down the street and is confronted by another man with a gun. He points the gun at him and demands his wallet. What do you think he would do? Most would assume he would give the man his wallet. If the logical reaction to a criminal with a gun is compliance, why then, when the person holding the gun is a police officer, is compliance not also the logical reaction?

Another claim Black Lives Matter and its followers make is that white people can disobey commands and attack the police and not get shot. They say whites get arrested, but "we" get shot. This is the weakest of their arguments. Even a cursory Google search will produce plenty of examples of black people who attacked police officers without being shot, and plenty of whites who have been shot by police. They use church mass murderer Dylann Roof as an example of a white killer who was arrested.

---

32 Bayliss Wagner, "Fact check: Ma'Khia Bryant was holding a knife when shot by police," *USA Today*, April 21, 2021. https://www.usatoday.com/story/news/factcheck/2021/04/21/fact-check-makhia-bryant-holding-knife-while-shot-columbus-police/7321951002/

I guess they have forgotten about the D.C. Snipers,[33] Ronnie DeWayne Kato Jr.,[34] and Edward Archer,[35] all of whom are black, and all of whom were arrested—even though the latter two attacked police.

Each police interaction is different: different officer, different suspect, different circumstances. You would never know that by listening to the media. They have a narrative they want to portray—due either to their beliefs or the push for ratings—but they seize upon the "white cop, black victim" incidents as peddled by Black Lives Matter. This is why so many believe the media is part of the problem. In 2019, fifty-four people were shot and killed by police nationwide; twenty-three were black. In 2020, police shot and killed fifty-five unarmed men nationwide; twenty-three were black.[36] It may come as a surprise to many

---

33 Matthew Barakat (contributor), "DC Sniper's US Supreme court case dropped due to Virginia law change," Associated Press story, *Chicago Sun-Times*, February 26, 2020. https://chicago.suntimes.com/2020/2/26/21155413/dc-snipers-lee-boyd-malvo-supreme-court-case-dropped-virginia-law-ralph-northam

34 Janet McConnaughey and Claudia Lauer, "Police: Man ambushed officer; stood over body, kept shooting," Associated Press story, WWLTV.com, April 27, 2020. https://www.wwltv.com/article/news/crime/police-man-ambushed-officer-stood-over-body-kept-shooting/289-e9735b02-4635-449a-8874-1d0aed7f4bf1

35 "Edward Archer sentenced up to 97 years in prison for shooting of Officer Jesse Hartnett in name of ISIS," CBSN Philly, March 14, 2018. https://philadelphia.cbslocal.com/2018/05/14/sentencing-day-for-edward-archer-who-shot-philadelphia-officer-jesse-hartnett-in-name-of-isis/

36 "Fatal force: 990 people were shot and killed by police in 2018," *The Washington Post,* database updated June 1, 2020. https://www.washingtonpost.com/graphics/2018/national/police-shootings-2018/

people that the majority of those killed by police were white. It is also interesting to note that despite the higher number of police killings being white men, all of the highly publicized police shooting are of black men. I would challenge anyone—outside of family or friends—to name one of the white men killed by police in 2020.

Finally, we are constantly told that black parents must teach their children how to act when confronted by police and white parents do not. We are then told that police are more likely to shoot black men than white men. If this is true, why do so many black men, when confronted by a "racist cop with a gun" and after being trained for years on how to act, choose to disregard orders or, in some cases, attack the officer?

Let me clearly state that every police shooting should be investigated, and all officers found to have used force improperly or excessively should be prosecuted. But each situation is different, and acting as if police shootings of unarmed blacks is an "epidemic," or placing the blame solely on the police officer, is both foolish and counterproductive.

Police brutality exists but is most likely displayed in threats or assaults. This should be the focus of reforms, but Black Lives Matter only talks about shootings. This is key to finding a solution. The perceived level of a problem will dictate how quickly action will be taken as well as how drastic that action will be. Black Lives Matter's extreme positions on police, like defunding them or in some cases abolishing them, and its constant assertion that there is a "war on black people," do not comport with the facts.

Harvard economics professor Roland G. Fryer, Jr. did an empirical analysis of racial differences in police use of force.[37] His comprehensive study examined over 1,300 shootings spanning fifteen years in ten cities. The study found that "In shootings in these 10 cities involving officers, officers were more likely to fire their weapons without having first been attacked when the suspects were white."

His study did not stop there. He went on to examine situations where the officers had sufficient reason to use lethal force but did not. He determined this by looking at arrest reports and examining cases where the suspects shot at the officers, resisted arrest, or tried to physically attack the officers. Mr. Fryer found that in such situations, officers in Houston were about 20 percent less likely to shoot if the suspects were black.

The marchers and protesters all claim that police officers killing unarmed black men is an epidemic, despite all evidence showing that claim is a fallacy. You can look at an individual shooting and determine that officer was wrong, but even if every shooting were wrong, it still would not make the case for an epidemic. In the sixteen years of Fryer's study, 1.6 million total arrests were made, and officers fired their weapons only 507 times. This is consistent all over the country. Yet uninformed athletes and biased journalists shape the narrative.

Even if we ignore the overwhelming amount of evidence to the contrary and assume Black Lives Matter are right—even if my interpretation of the data is wrong, and police brutality is the

---

[37] Quoctrung Bui and Amanda Cox, "Surprising new evidence shows bias in police use of force but not in shootings," *New York Times*, July 11, 2016. https://www.nytimes.com/2016/07/12/upshot/surprising-new-evidence-shows-bias-in-police-use-of-force-but-not-in-shootings.html

existential threat for blacks that Black Lives Matter and others are declaring—the proposals on their website and the actions they're participating in still don't address the problems they are decrying. These organizations like to describe their problems as mortal, but their solutions are, well, less solution and more abstract feelings. They claim to be an organization focused on blacks, but their focus has little to do with actually improving the lives of blacks.

For instance, the Black Lives Matter Foundation's stated mission is "to eradicate white supremacy and build local power to intervene in violence inflicted on Black communities by the state and vigilantes…." What is interesting here is that what we hear on the news, at the marches, and in their comments is all about police brutality; but here, they have added "vigilantes." I assume this was to acknowledge that George Zimmerman did not represent "the state" and to allow for rare situations like the death of Ahmaud Arbery. Arbery was a black man killed by a white father and son. They claimed he was committing a crime, and they were trying to make a citizens' arrest. The murder happened in February of 2020, and no arrest was made until May, only after a video was released of the incident.

While this situation is concerning and deserves the investigation it is finally getting, it is inconsistent with the Black Lives Matter argument. Vigilantism is not a prevailing issue in the country at large, let alone the black community. In fact, it is likely that most Black Lives Matter supporters cannot name one case where a black person was killed by a vigilante in the past year.

The common reply I get to this argument is that the Arbery case is only being investigated because there is video of it; therefore, there are likely many others we do not know about. While it is true that the arrests in this case would be unlikely without the video, assuming there are other vigilante murders is far-fetched and based on nothing.

The bottom line on police brutality is that it exists and must be rooted out where possible. Officers with little regard for the rights of the citizens they are sworn to protect, or who treat citizens differently based on any immutable trait, are abhorrent to their fellow officers and the country. However, creating a national movement around this, as if it is the prevailing issue in the black community, is factually inaccurate and worsens the already fractured relationship between the police and the public.

One last point about police brutality. If Black Lives Matter were genuinely concerned with the problem of police shootings, they would focus on all police shootings of unarmed men, not just the ones involving black victims. Instead, they ignore potential allies to focus on an enemy that does not exist. Here is one last number to consider: 2,115,381. That is the number of blacks who were arrested in 2018.[38]

If you count every black person killed by police that year, not just the twenty-two unarmed men—though many of the others attacked or shot at officers—the total is approximately 200 people. This is less than 1/100 of one percent of total blacks arrested, which is but a fraction of all blacks in America.

---

[38] Federal Bureau of Investigation, "Crime in the United States 2018," *Uniform Crime Reports*, U.S. Department of Justice, Table 43. https://ucr.fbi.gov/crime-in-the-u.s/2018/crime-in-the-u.s.-2018/tables/table-43

There is no epidemic of racist police shootings, and Black Lives Matter would do better to use their energy and influence to try to have a positive impact on a more pressing issue in the black community. But that wouldn't advance their agenda.

2

Black in Name Only

No one would deny that the black community faces complicated issues. There are various reasons for these issues, and they have remained unaddressed for so long that they have metastasized. Solving these problems will be difficult and will take years to repair. The government has its role to play in the solutions, but can only do so much. The community must bring us the rest of the way.

An organization like Black Lives Matter should be a force for good in the community. Unfortunately, their approach is bad, and in the ways that count, they are nowhere to be seen in the black community.

The problems that blacks face in low-income neighborhoods are on display daily. They are discussed at community meetings and public hearings across the country, but Black Lives Matter is rarely part of these conversations. They fan the flames of police hatred but rarely take an active role in improving conditions for those struggling in the community. And if their absence in the community wasn't bad enough, many blacks are beginning to point out that they have not seen any signs of the millions of dollars Black Lives Matters has collected on their behalf.[39]

To understand what Black Lives Matter has become, we must examine their ideology, in their own words. Black Lives Matter's stated mission is "to eradicate white supremacy and build local power to intervene in violence inflicted on Black communities by the state and vigilantes. By combating and countering acts of violence, creating space for Black imagination and innovation, and centering Black joy, we are winning immediate improvements in our lives."

This statement is brilliant in saying nothing while making you feel something. Who can be against creating spaces for black imagination and innovation? A better question may be what does this mean, and how can it be executed? The last part of the mission is to eradicate white supremacy. Here is a goal I can get behind. Unfortunately, even the goals that are not misguided are exaggerated and impossible to achieve.

If they mean white supremacy in the way most people would understand it, how do you eradicate it? It is a feeling or belief within an individual. It is misguided and evil, but it is not something the government can legislate, or a pseudo-charity can "eradicate." I believe their meaning of white supremacy is based on an often-assumed self-inferiority among blacks. They must believe that whites are superior because they aim to diminish a supremacy whites do not actually have.

---

39 Maya King, "Black Lives Matter power grab sets off internal revolt," *Politico*, December 10, 2020. https://www.politico.com/news/2020/12/10/black-lives-matter-organization-biden-444097

This twisted perspective starts with the mission statement but extends throughout the Black Lives Matter website. Much of it consists of empty platitudes, manufactured villains, and dangerous rhetoric. The remainder are social issues that read like the 2020 Democratic Party platform.

The "What We Believe" section is where Black Lives Matter details the core values of the organization. No matter whether you agree with its feel-good emptiness or not, after analyzing each point it will be undeniable that the organization is not focused on the black community or police brutality. Here are their planks:

> *We acknowledge, respect, and celebrate differences and commonalities.*

Here, what they mean by "differences" are clearly limited. It is evident that differences in political, economic, or religious views are not respected or celebrated. After all, white supremacists have differences and commonalities. Are they celebrated? They may do better limiting the differences they "celebrate" to the ones specifically listed on their webpage.

> *We work vigorously for freedom and justice for Black people and, by extension, all people.*

Here again, is a contradiction in terms. How can one "vigorously" work for freedom and justice for black people and think that will automatically extend to "all" people? By prioritizing a specific group, you will inevitably discriminate against another.

> *We intentionally build and nurture a beloved community that is bonded together through a beautiful struggle that is restorative, not depleting.*

Most of this is just rhetoric designed to imbue happy feelings akin to a mother's love. It means nothing and does not even address black lives. The one word that is important here is "restorative." Whenever a "social justice" group says the word *restorative*, they mean it in the most unequal sense. It means taking something from its rightful owner and "returning" it to someone who has no rightful claim to it.

> *We are unapologetically Black in our positioning. In affirming that Black Lives Matter, we need not qualify our position. To love and desire freedom and justice for ourselves is a prerequisite for wanting the same for others.*

The issue here is more nuanced. It is fine for them to proclaim their blackness, and they should not apologize. And while qualifying their position is not necessary, clarifying it seems warranted. For instance, does black positioning mean there is consensus amongst blacks on what that positioning looks like? Also, in affirming that Black Lives Matter, are they including all black lives?

They mention many struggles in black life, but there is not a single mention of abortion, crime, or education. Aborted babies and victims of violent crime are disproportionately black; so are the children failed by public school education in many cities across the country; yet none of these is affirmed or even acknowledged.

While crime has been an ongoing problem in the inner cities, black-on-black crime has been a point of contention in the black community. This is not what I am talking about. I am less concerned in this context with who commits the crime than I am with the victims. Black men are the vast majority of gun-violence victims in the U.S. with over 4,000 murders in 2019. They are more likely to commit a violent crime or be a victim of one. This is a crucial issue within the black community and should be high on the priority list of anyone addressing problems in black America.

When discussing crime as it relates to black women, the most shocking issue is that so many disappear with little outcry. In 2019, *Medium* published the article, "There Are 64,000 Missing Black Women in the USA."[40] This should be seen as an epidemic, yet it is largely unknown to most Americans, including the black community. The article states:

> "Even though they are not the majority of the population, at approximately 13 percent, black people often make up a significant percentage of missing persons at around 30 percent—making them overrepresented in terms of going missing.... African-American missing persons cases are often older and left open, with black children being more likely to remain missing than white or hispanic [sic] children when looking at the same time span."

---

[40] Samantha Clarke, "There are 64,000 missing black women in the USA," *Medium*, November 23, 2019. https://medium.com/the-blight/there-are-64-000-missing-black-women-in-the-usa-222001806a6e

Public schools have been failing black children for decades: from the Atlanta cheating scandal[41] and NYC's abysmal testing scores[42] to the Chicago sex scandal,[43] all these mostly affect black children. These issues—abortion, crime, and education—greatly diminish the quality of life for many black people, yet none of them are addressed on the Black Lives Matter website.

> *We see ourselves as part of the global Black family, and we are aware of the different ways we are impacted or privileged as Black people who exist in different parts of the world.*

What is interesting here is that with all of their talk about "privilege" and their constant complaints of systemic inequalities, they acknowledged, perhaps in a moment of clarity, that blacks in America are more privileged than blacks in other parts of the world.

> *We are guided by the fact that all Black lives matter, regardless of actual or perceived sexual identity,*

---

41 WXIA-TV, "11 Atlanta educators convicted in cheating scandal," *USA Today*, April 1, 2015. https://www.usatoday.com/story/news/nation/2015/04/01/atlanta-schools-cheating-scandal-verdict/70780606/

42 Selim Algar, "Over 140 NYC schools have grades with 90 percent state exam failure rate," *New York Post*, December 17, 2019. https://nypost.com/2019/12/17/over-140-nyc-schools-have-grades-with-90-percent-state-exam-failure-rate/

43 "CPS sex abuse report: District failed to protect students victimized by teachers, workers," CBSN Chicago, August 17, 2018. https://chicago.cbslocal.com/2018/08/17/cps-sex-abuse-report/

> *gender identity, gender expression, economic status, ability, disability, religious beliefs or disbeliefs, immigration status, or location.*

Earlier, they were celebrating differences and commonalities; now they are saying that all of these different statuses of people are equal, so long as they are black. Also of note, they made sure they included every possible subset of black person—"actual or perceived sexual identity," "religious beliefs or disbeliefs," even "location"—but they could not find room for political ideology.

> *We make space for transgender brothers and sisters to participate and lead.*

In this short, rather innocuous sentence, they made a powerful statement about their priorities. Being inclusive can be commended. However, there seems to be a special place in the organization, especially leadership, for trans people and women. Take notice, as this is the first but not the last time this will be prioritized.

> *We are self-reflexive [sic]and do the work required to dismantle cisgender privilege and uplift Black trans folk, especially Black trans women who continue to be disproportionately impacted by trans-antagonistic violence.*

The average person will see this and likely have no idea what they're talking about. For most, this is the first time they have seen the word "cisgender" before. To simplify, they feel that heterosexual people have privilege, and it is necessary to suppress it.

What's troubling is not their affirmation of transgender people, but their open disdain for heterosexual people.

No rational person condones violence on anyone, including transgender people, and I cannot say whether black trans women are disproportionately impacted by violence. Still, I do know this has nothing to do with "cisgender privilege." For a group who constantly reminds you they were "born this way," can't the rest of us say the same thing?

If you are paying attention, you are starting to see a trend. These guiding principles have little to do with the group's original goal of combating police brutality. This is a recurring issue throughout the website, and where most fair-minded people start to realize Black Lives Matter has become less about black lives and more about an ideological political platform.

> *We build a space that affirms Black women and is free from sexism, misogyny, and environments in which men are centered.*

I wanted to find a principle I could agree with and thought this would be it. I too appreciate a space that is free from sexism and misogyny, but the last part is troubling. Why are environments in which men are centered a bad thing? If men were exclusively allowed to be at the center, this affirmation would make sense, but how can it be bad simply to have men at the center of the organization? Also, they expressed their aversion to gender bias earlier but now are committing themselves to gender bias.

> *We practice empathy. We engage comrades with the intent to learn about and connect with their contexts.*

This is another principle that is just word candy, but I am always leery when I hear people described as "comrades." It hearkens back to Marx's *Communist Manifesto* or Mao's *Little Red Book*.

> *We make our spaces family-friendly and enable parents to fully participate with their children. We dismantle the patriarchal practice that requires mothers to work "double shifts" so that they can mother in private even as they participate in public justice work.*

It is unclear what patriarchal practice they are referring to, but I don't believe one exists that requires mothers to work double shifts. In fact, it could be argued that a patriarchal society would want women out of the workforce. In any event, this is another belief that is solely focused on women. They imply that either men are not concerned about black lives or have little respect for women.

> *We disrupt the Western-prescribed nuclear family structure requirement by supporting each other as extended families and "villages" that collectively care for one another, especially our children, to the degree that mothers, parents, and children are comfortable.*

This is the most confusing and distressing of all of their guiding principles. One of the few things that most blacks agree on, regardless of background or political ideology, is that the nuclear family is a child's best chance for success in life. It can predict school success, college completion, and income level, as well as avoidance of prison and drug usage. So, why would an organization wholly focused on black lives be against the nuclear family? They must be called to answer for promoting this belief.

> *We foster a queer-affirming network. When we gather, we do so with the intention of freeing ourselves from the tight grip of heteronormative thinking, or rather, the belief that all in the world are heterosexual (unless s/he or they disclose otherwise).*

Black Lives Matter is obsessed with gender; that alone should be troubling. But there seems to be an unhealthy obsession with creating the illusion that heterosexuality is not the norm. In fact, in their view, it is problematic to believe that most of the world is heterosexual. I do not know what a queer-affirming network is, but I do know from surveys by Pew and Gallup that about 95 percent of people are heterosexual; so why wouldn't people assume others they meet are heterosexual unless they disclose otherwise?

> *We cultivate an intergenerational and communal network free from ageism. We believe that all people, regardless of age, show up with the capacity to lead and learn.*

Again, they almost had my complete agreement. Cultivating an intergenerational network and operating without ageism is not an issue. Unfortunately, extremists cannot help being extreme. How can all people, regardless of age, lead? I do not believe a four-year-old would be capable of leading, but then again, with the mindless drivel provided so far, perhaps children *are* leading them.

> *We embody and practice justice, liberation, and peace in our engagements with one another.*

I cannot argue with this one. Although I wish that the peace they practice with one another would be extended to the rest of society.

All the previous italicized points are direct quotes from their website. Keep in mind, they may be updated at any time. When I started writing, I copied the "What We Believe" page. Here is an excerpt that is no longer available:

> Black Lives Matter is an ideological and political intervention in a world where Black lives are systematically and intentionally targeted for demise. It is an affirmation of Black folks' humanity, our contributions to this society, and our resilience in the face of deadly oppression.
>
> As a network, we have always recognized the need to center the leadership of women and queer and trans people. To maximize our movement muscle, and to be intentional about not replicating harmful practices that excluded so many in past movements for liberation, we made a commitment to placing those at the margins closer to the center.

I am not sure why they removed it. It is no more extreme than the other expressed beliefs. Perhaps they did not want to admit they were a political organization in an election year. Although most can tell by their actions that they are. It is a bit shocking to say that blacks are targeted for demise or that they face "deadly oppression." The last paragraph was likely removed due to repetition rather than shame. In any event, these were accurate at the time of this writing, and changing the page does not change their beliefs.

The last example of their lack of focus on the black community is the "Global Actions" page. One would expect to see a list of wonderful accomplishments they have made around the world in this section. Instead, it was a timeline of one story. The page should be renamed the 21 Savage Fan Club.

21 Savage is a Grammy Award–winning rapper who had come to fame from his hometown of Atlanta, Georgia. On February 3, 2019, he was riding in a car with his cousin, rapper Young Nudy, real name Quantavious Thomas. Thomas was arrested and charged with aggravated assault and violation of the Georgia Gang Act. Subsequently, 21 Savage was arrested by ICE (Immigration and Customs Enforcement). It was determined he was a United Kingdom national who had overstayed his nonimmigrant visa.[44]

Black Lives Matter spent the next ten days fighting to get 21 Savage released. They gathered signatures, petitioned elected officials, and wrote the immigration judge advocating for his

[44] Matthew Strauss, "21 Savage's ICE detention allegedly instigated by the arrest of his cousin Nudy," *Pitchfork,* February 4, 2019. https://pitchfork.com/news/21-savage-ice-detention-allegedly-instigated-by-the-arrest-of-his-cousin-young-nudy/

release. Black Lives Matter activists demonstrated outside the Grammys and organized phone calls to Sean Gallagher, the ICE Field Office Director. Finally, they released a PSA with several celebrities, including Mike Tyson and Kendrick Lamar, supporting 21 Savage. He was eventually released.

This is the one win on the Global Actions page. While I am sure 21 Savage appreciates their efforts, this does not seem like a win for black people. It may support celebrity privilege or undocumented immigrant privilege, but it does nothing for the people they claim to be fighting to help. One must ask why Black Lives Matter thinks focusing on one person residing in the country illegally aligns with their mission.

This is where the now-removed statement about political intervention starts to make sense. When going through the principles on their What We Believe page, I made several comments about the lack of focus on police brutality or any other issues facing black America. Looking at the beliefs through a political lens, though, everything they addressed aligns perfectly with a leftist political ideology. Knowing this makes it obvious that Black Lives Matter is not a black-focused organization. Don't take my word for it; listen to Dr. Claud Anderson.

Dr. Anderson is president of The Harvest Institute, a nationally recognized think tank that does research, policy development, education, and advocacy to increase the self-sufficiency of Black America.[45] He is the author of *Black Labor, White Wealth: The Search for Power and Economic Justice* and *PowerNomics: The National Plan to Empower Black America.* He was State Coordinator of Education for Florida under Governor Reubin Askew and the federal co-chairman for a commission of gov-

---

45 The Harvest Institute website: http://www.harvestinstitute.org/

ernors in the Southeast states. He testified before Congress on September 15, 2000, on the importance of reparations for black Americans.[46] No one can question his concern for black America.

He recently wrote a paper outlining the problems immigration policy has on the black community. He argues that America's policies have given aid to immigrants to the detriment of black Americans. Commenting on the report, he said, "These civil rights leaders keep talking about we're all together as brothers. Those are not your brothers. They are coming here to compete with you. You are in a race. In a race you don't try to get along with everybody, you try to get ahead."[47]

The bottom line is that there are generally two schools of thought in addressing the black community's issues. One is the conservative view; this belief is that the solutions will come from the community itself. The focus is on personal responsibility, making wise decisions, a charitable community, educational achievement, and an entrepreneurial spirit.

The liberal view focuses on the respective roles of government and capitalism. It holds that the government has failed the black community and has a duty to play a large part in fixing it. Many of the issues, this approach contends, are caused by systemic problems and greedy corporations that prey on the poor. Racism is also a huge component here.

While these views are quite different and blacks who hold the competing views often have contentious arguments, I believe

---

[46] Dr. Claud Anderson, Testimony Before U.S. House Judiciary Committee, September 15, 2000. Video archived online at: https://www.youtube.com/watch?v=_IAkp2O_dBk

[47] Boyce Watkins interview of Dr. Claud Anderson, *"Dr. Boyce TV,"* The Black Business School, January 31, 2019. Video archived online at https://www.youtube.com/watch?v=mm7f9jvzTV0

they both genuinely care about the black community. Black Lives Matter does not fall in either category. On the surface, it may seem that they are aligned with the second group described above. Therefore, it is important to analyze their beliefs in their own words.

While there may be disagreement within the community on what to do to solve the problems, every respectable organization focused on the black community mentions these and other problems. Black Lives Matter not only ignores large issues within the black community, they rarely mention police brutality anymore—no statistics, no facts, and no solutions. Currently, the site is focused on an MLK artist series, ending the federal 1033 program, which transfers excess military equipment to civilian law enforcement agencies, and the BLM Survival Fund.[48]

The fund, they claim, was created to help blacks during the pandemic but the site states, "The BLM Survival Fund has met its goal of providing direct support to nearly 3,000 Black people and their families, and we will be closing applications until further notice." Ninety million dollars and they can only help 3,000 people?

For this to be their *raison d'être*, it is interesting to see it take a backseat to LGBTQ issues and undocumented people. Their dedication of a full page to an undocumented immigrant is just one of many examples of their disregard for the black community.[49]

48 Defense Logistics Agency, "1033 Program FAQs," DLA Disposition Services, n.d. https://www.dla.mil/DispositionServices/Offers/Reutilization/LawEnforcement/ProgramFAQs.aspx

49 Black Lives Matter, "Global Actions - February 2019: #Free21Savage," n.d. https://blacklivesmatter.com/global-actions/

Even with internal problems coming to light, Black Lives Matter enjoys tremendous support across the country, including overwhelming support within the black community. When challenged on the efficacy of Black Lives Matter, many argue that no organization is perfect. While true, it is likely they do not know the extent to which Black Lives Matter is fighting against their interests. It is imperative that those of us who see the damage Black Lives Matter is doing to the country communicate this message to the masses. With a clearer understanding of what they believe and what their goals are, most Americans, including black Americans, will see there is little upon which they agree with Black Lives Matter.

3

Is Violence the Answer?

COVID-19 and its accompanying lockdowns have ushered us into a new way of life. While we hope it is temporary, everyone has had to adjust. In areas where indoor dining was still forbidden, a leisurely alfresco meal was the closest thing to pre-viral life and a way to enjoy the company of family or friends. So, imagine the shock and horror Washington D.C. diners felt when they were accosted by Black Lives Matter protestors.

On a Tuesday night in late August 2020, a group of protesters descended on diners at a D.C. restaurant. The incident was caught on tape by *Washington Post* reporter Fredrick Kunkle.[50] The protesters attempted to force the restaurant's patrons to raise

[50] N'dea Yancey-Bragg, "Viral videos show Black Lives Matter protesters confronting diners in Washington, D.C.," *USA Today,* August 26, 2020. https://www.usatoday.com/story/news/nation/2020/08/26/video-black-lives-matter-protest-confronting-dc-diners-goes-viral/3441636001/

their fists in solidarity with Black Lives Matter while chanting refrains like, "White silence is violence" and "No justice, no peace." Unfortunately, scenes like these are becoming common in many big cities.

Black Lives Matter is no longer the organization it was created to be. While many still associate the catchy name with police brutality, BLM has shifted from being a grassroots organization with that narrowly defined albeit misguided purpose, to becoming a dangerous mouthpiece for a broad leftist political agenda. While they do little to promote solutions, Black Lives Matter has done a lot to sow discord in a country they believe to be evil to its core. In waging this ideologically driven war on America, they ironically exemplify everything they and their followers accuse their opposition of being, routinely using violent language, threats, and acts to get their way.

As violent protests increase in U.S. cities, Black Lives Matter and their allies encourage them, excuse them, or turn a blind eye to them.[51] Hawk Newsome, Black Lives Matter Greater NY said, "If this country doesn't give us what we want, then we will burn down this system and replace it." He coyly told Fox News host Martha MacCallum, "…and I could be speaking figuratively, I could be speaking literally. It's a matter of interpretation."[52]

---

[51] Amitai Etzioni, "The Black Lives Matter movement must solve its violence problem," *The National Interest*, June 29, 2020. https://nationalinterest.org/feature/black-lives-matter-movement-must-solve-its-violence-problem-163732

[52] Victor Garcia, "Black Lives Matter leader states if US 'doesn't give us what we want, then we will burn down this system,'" FoxNews.com, June 24, 2020. https://www.foxnews.com/media/black-lives-matter-leader-burn-down-system

When you encourage the mob, you get more mob action. In Chicago, after it was falsely reported that the police had shot a fifteen-year-old fifteen times, hundreds of young, mostly black protestors, took to the streets. They looted high-end stores across the main shopping districts. Ariel Atkins from Black Lives Matter Chicago condoned the looting, calling it "reparations." She told WBEZ, Chicago's NPR station, "The whole idea of criminality is based on racism anyway." She continued, "Because criminality is punishing people for things that they have needed to do to survive or just the way that society has affected them with white supremacist BS."[53]

In Seattle, Black Lives Matter activists attacked a local news reporter who was trying to record a protest; a second reporter was also harassed.[54] Black Lives Matter Louisville threatened to attack or shut down businesses that didn't comply with their demands.[55]

Meanwhile, police continue to be attacked across the country. In New York City shortly after George Floyd's death, two lawyers were arrested for throwing a Molotov cocktail into a

---

[53] Rob Wildeboer and Chip Mitchell, "Winning has come through revolts: A Black Lives Matter activist on why she supports looting," WBEZ Chicago, August 12, 2020. https://www.wbez.org/stories/winning-has-come-through-revolts-a-black-lives-matter-activist-on-why-she-supports-looting/398d0f3f-73d0-4f2e-ae32-04cceba0d322

[54] Julio Rosas, "Black Lives Matter mob surrounds and threaten local Seattle news crew," Townhall.com, August 20, 2020. https://townhall.com/tipsheet/juliorosas/2020/08/20/black-lives-matter-mob-surrounds-and-threaten-local-seattle-news-crew-n2574770

[55] Bailey Loosemore, "Cuban community plans rally at Nulu restaurant in response to Black Lives Matter demands," *Louisville Courier Journal*, August 1, 2020; updated August 3, 2020. https://www.courier-journal.com/story/news/local/2020/08/01/louisville-cuban-community-rally-support-la-bodeguita-de-mima/5562669002/

police vehicle.[56] Police stations were burned in Minneapolis and taken over in Seattle. After a black man was shot by police in Kenosha, Wisconsin, a police officer was knocked unconscious while protestors cheered.

BLM's broader leftist political agenda became unmistakably clear last year in its choice of political targets. After the Republican National Convention in Washington, D.C., people were mobbed, threatened, and harassed by Black Lives Matter activists. Among the attendees attacked were Vernon Jones, a Georgia state representative who, as a black man and Democrat, endorsed President Trump, and Alice Johnson, the black woman President Trump pardoned after her case was brought to his attention by Kim Kardashian West. People whose only crime was attending an event for the sitting president of the United States were aggressively confronted on American streets.[57]

The attack that paints the best picture of the fact that these protestors are misguided and uninformed is that of Senator Rand Paul and his wife. The mob could be heard saying, "Say

---

[56] William K. Rashbaum and Andrea Salcedo, "Two lawyers arrested in Molotov cocktail attack on police in Brooklyn," *The New York Times*, May 31, 2020. https://www.nytimes.com/2020/05/31/nyregion/nyc-protests-lawyer-molotov-cocktail.html

[57] Andrea Mark Miller, "Vernon Jones calls on Democrats to investigate after BLM mob swarms him outside GOP convention," *Washington Examiner*, August 29, 2020. https://www.washingtonexaminer.com/news/vernon-jones-calls-on-democrats-to-investigate-after-blm-mob-swarms-him-outside-gop-convention

her name!" and "What about Breonna!"[58] It was a reference to Breonna Taylor, the woman killed by police during a raid. Taylor was killed in Louisville, the state where Rand Paul is a U.S. Senator. Yet there is a confusing aspect to their rage.

In June, just two months before the convention, Senator Paul introduced the Justice for Breonna Taylor Act in honor of Taylor. At the time, Senator Paul said, "After talking with Breonna Taylor's family, I've concluded that it is long past time to get rid of no-knock warrants. This bill will effectively end no-knock raids in the United States." So not only did he say her name, he spoke to her family and authored a bill in her honor. But why let facts get in the way of mob action? If Black Lives Matter's real objective was the betterment of the black community, why target a political figure who promoted legislation that supports their demands? However, if BLM's real objective is tearing down the American capitalist system, then attacking a prominent Republican makes perfect sense.

When they are not threatening people, demanding whites give up their homes,[59] or trying to force unsuspecting diners to raise their fists in solidarity with Black Lives Matter, they are claiming racism everywhere they can. Whenever there is a

---

58 Ian Schwartz, "Rand Paul attacked by protesters: Without police, people will be pummeled senseless on the curb," *RealClearPolitics*, August 28, 2020. https://www.realclearpolitics.com/video/2020/08/28/rand_paul_attacked_by_protesters_without_police_people_will_be_pummeled_senseless_on_the_curb.html

59 Erin Van Der Meer, "'Give up your house': Black Lives Matter activists storm neighborhood and demand white residents give up their homes," *The Sun*, August 15, 2020. https://www.thesun.co.uk/news/12406818/blm-activists-seattle-white-residents-give-up-homes/

perceived injustice, usually based on insufficient facts and questionable logic, they are ready with a popup protest.

They are not the only ones who are complicit in encouraging, even participating in, urban violence; the media are also adding to the problem as enablers and excuse-makers. Some of the media bias on behalf of Black Lives Matter lies in the language media outlets use to frame news stories.

For example, when the Proud Boys, an alleged right-wing group, organized a rally in Michigan, a fight broke out. This is how it was described in the *U.S. Sun*: "A rally organized by far-right group Proud Boys in Kalamazoo, Michigan, escalated into violence when they were met by counter-protesters and 'Antifa members.'"[60]

Pay close attention to the deception. The Proud Boys are "far-right" but Antifa is not "far-left." In addition, Antifa is presented as a group separate from other counter-protestors. This is a common media tactic. Basically, if Black Lives Matter is clearly to blame for violence, the media typically will blame only the single member at fault. However, if a right-wing organization or a white person is to blame, then *all* conservatives, Republicans, and Donald Trump are depicted as being at fault.

There also has been a deliberate attempt, fostered by the media, to separate Black Lives Matter from Antifa. This is becoming increasingly more difficult to do, since so many violent protests include members of both groups. I cannot say whether the groups have merged, but what we know is they both have the

---

60 Lucy Sherriff, "LEFT VS. RIGHT: Shocking moment right-wing Proud Boys group and Antifa protesters brawl during ugly clash in Michigan," *The Sun*, August 17, 2020. https://www.the-sun.com/news/1316052/proud-boys-group-brawl-antifa-protests-kalamazoo-michigan/

same enemies, speak the same language, use violence, and talk obsessively about race. Antifa used to have a larger focus on class warfare; but even on that point the two groups are ideologically aligned. Patrisse Cullors, a co-founder of Black Lives Matter and its interim board president, made their beliefs clear when she famously said, "We are trained Marxists."[61]

The problem with connecting the two groups is that there is no real leadership. For example, Black Lives Matter came out to say that Hank Newsome, the New York BLM advocate who earlier called for violence, is not a spokesperson for the group. However, this dispute seems more personal than ideological, as they have not condemned anyone else for committing crimes or making outrageous statements in the group's name. (In the next section, I will explain the organizational structure of the movement, and you will see why it is as hard to connect Black Lives Matter to the fringe actors as it is for them to separate themselves from them.)

In any event, Black Lives Matter is similar to Antifa in that it has no real purpose besides wreaking havoc and tearing down the country. Demanding redistribution of wealth or equity over equality is not the talk of serious advocates for positive change. Instead of offering solutions, these groups opt to divide the country along racial and socioeconomic lines and chant "feel good" rhetoric that attracts those with little understanding of the unique freedoms on which this country was founded.

---

[61] Yaron Steinbuch, "Black Lives Matter co-founder describes herself as 'trained Marxist,'" *New York Post*, June 25, 2020. https://nypost.com/2020/06/25/blm-co-founder-describes-herself-as-trained-marxist/

Take the most common refrain heard during the protests: "No justice, no peace!" It may seem morally proper, but this phrase is born out of anger and aggression, and its vile intentions are quite clear. They are saying that they want to intimidate Americans and make them uncomfortable and fearful until whatever they call "justice" is served. There is a fundamental problem with both parts of this slogan.

First, they do not want justice, they want their Marxist *idea* of justice. As I laid out earlier, justice was served in Michael Brown's death, but they continue to invoke his name, falsely, as a victim of a police murder. If the standard for justice is set by the mob, they will never be satisfied. Derek Chauvin was found guilty on all charges in the death of George Floyd, yet many on the left, including Congresswoman Alexandria Ocasio-Cortez, proclaimed, "This verdict is not justice."[62]

The other part of their decree is that if you fall short of completely capitulating to their skewed idea of justice, you will not be allowed to live peacefully. It is amazing that there are people who claim to believe in freedom that agree with this, but many of our leaders in corporate America, the media, and politics applaud this slogan and its advocates. For instance, while campaigning last year, then Democratic vice-presidential nominee Kamala Harris said about BLM in an interview with Stephen

---

[62] Haley Victory Smith, "'This verdict is not justice': AOC reacts to Derek Chauvin conviction," *Washington Examiner*, April 20, 2021. https://www.washingtonexaminer.com/news/verdict-justice-aoc-derek-chauvin-conviction

Colbert, "They're not going to let up, and they shouldn't."[63] Congresswoman Maxine Waters made a similar claim about members of the Trump administration; then, in the wake of the Chauvin trial, upped the ante by telling protestors to "get more confrontational" if Chauvin is found not guilty.[64]

What they fail to understand is that protestors' freedom ceases when it encroaches on the rights of others. Our natural rights, and those listed in the Declaration of Independence and protected in the Constitution, guarantee life, liberty, and the pursuit of happiness. Contrary to their slogan, threatening others' lives and deliberately suppressing their pursuit of happiness is fostering *injustice*. When your elderly neighbor must commute an extra fifteen minutes to get her prescription because her pharmacy has been burned down in the name of "justice," that is both an injustice and a fraudulent use of language. Those who say this is necessary discomfort to affect change are being disingenuous. If that were the case, we could be ordered to give up comforts to end human trafficking, poverty, heart disease, and every other "good cause" anyone decides to assert. This is no way to lead a justice-based movement.

It is clear why Black Lives Matter activists participate in violent, racist behavior; it works. Black Lives Matter activists have screamed at diners, attacked police, suborned looting, labeled

---

63 Camille Caldera, "Fact check: Kamala Harris said protests aren't going to stop, but condemns violence," *USA Today*, September 17, 2020. https://www.usatoday.com/story/news/factcheck/2020/09/01/fact-check-kamala-harris-said-protests-arent-going-stop/5678687002/

64 Chandelis Duster, "Waters calls for protesters to 'get more confrontational' if no guilty verdict is reached in Derek Chauvin trial," *CNN*, April 20, 2021. https://edition.cnn.com/2021/04/19/politics/maxine-waters-derek-chauvin-trial/index.html

all whites racist, and threatened to burn the system down—and the reaction to these behaviors has been millions of dollars in donations, the BLM logo alongside corporate ones, freedom to violate COVID-19 social distancing guidelines, and their false rhetoric and racist demands parroted by elected officials. With all the increased racial strife Black Lives Matter has caused, they are still driving the narrative on race in the country. Perhaps violence *is* the answer.

Some say we are headed for a race war. I disagree, as the makeup of the country makes that impossible. There are too many mixed-race people, immigrants, minority conservatives, leftist white elites, and BLM-Antifa members. If we were separated solely by race, you would have most Trump supporters and Hollywood celebrities on one side, and black conservatives and Black Lives Matter on the other. No matter the narrative people try to push, we simply cannot be divided that way.

Dennis Prager, nationally syndicated radio host and author of *The Rational Bible*, has a better take on the rift. He has long said that we are in a non-violent civil war, and he hopes it stays that way. I am unsure if it will remain non-violent, but whatever happens, the fight will be ideological, not racial. I believe the current phase is a series of political proxy wars. What Black Lives Matter is doing is operating on the behalf of the political left, and the current cultural climate is tailor-made for them.

Unfortunately, Black Lives Matter has gained so much mainstream support that it will be difficult to stop their momentum. Still, there is opportunity in the fact that few know their true intentions. This is why I work to educate people on what the movement really believes. If more people knew what they were about, support would wane. Even if they maintained support in some circles of society, corporations would be far less likely to openly support them.

As Black Lives Matter's prominence grew, many opponents began questioning their operations. How can they operate in such political ways and not be in violation of the rules surrounding nonprofit organizations? Where is their funding coming from, and how is it used? I decided to try to find the answer to these questions. What I found was that BLM existed within a mix of associated organizations and donors whose complexity and brazen dishonesty would have made Bernie Madoff blush.

There is a far more sinister organization at the helm of this movement. It controls messaging, provides funding, and promulgates extreme policy proposals designed to support and sustain this anti-American movement. Its danger is increased by the fact that it operates in relative anonymity. Everyone has an opinion on Black Lives Matter, and most people have at least heard of The 1619 Project. Yet I have mentioned this organization to radio personalities, journalists, academics, and politicians, and few have heard of them.

Now it's time we examine the Movement for Black Lives.

MOVEMENT FOR BLACK LIVES

4

ORGANIZATION AND FUNDING

If Black Lives Matter is the chaos arm of the movement, the Movement for Black Lives is the operating system. How a group so connected, so influential, and so well-funded can operate with no exposure in the age of social media is both a testament to its power and a sad statement of how far the media has fallen. Before I chronicle who they are and what they believe, I will explain the inadvertent way I found out about the group.

I was writing an article about Black Lives Matter and was clicking through their website to get some quotes. As I clicked through the site, something stood out to me. There was little information about the operation of the organization and absolutely no information on funding. There were no financial statements, no records of operational successes, and no list of a board of directors, other than Patrisse Cullors as interim board president.

This is a stark contrast to how most charity websites look. Regardless of size or scope, most charity websites supply financial reports and outline where the money goes; many even list large donors. Another prominent feature on most charity sites is their accomplishments and testimonials. The Fisher House will tell you how many families they housed near loved ones who have been hospitalized; Save the Children will tell you how your $300 donation will be spent; and Habitat for Humanity will tell you how many people had their homes built or improved. Black Lives Matter lists only their attempts to free 21 Savage.

I came up empty in my search for more information until I happened upon a 2016 article in the *Washington Times*. The article highlighted a $100 million grant Black Lives Matter received from liberal organizations.[65] It stated, "The Ford Foundation and Borealis Philanthropy recently announced the formation of the Black-Led Movement Fund [BLMF], a six-year pooled donor campaign aimed at raising $100 million for the Movement for Black Lives coalition."[66]

This only further confused me. I started with a search for Black Lives Matter's funding and found another organization; these funds were being raised for the Movement for Black Lives. That is a lot of money for a seemingly unknown organization. I was intrigued, so I kept digging. I clicked the link in the article for the Black-Led Movement Fund and was re-directed to a website for Borealis Philanthropy. There, I clicked a link to the Black-Led Movement Fund and got this as the fund's background:

---

65 Valerie Richardson, "Black Lives Matter cashes in with $100 million from liberal foundations," *Washington Times*, August 16, 2016. https://www.washingtontimes.com/news/2016/aug/16/black-lives-matter-cashes-100-million-liberal-foun/

66 The Borealis Philanthropy page listing its Black-Led Movement Fund: https://borealisphilanthropy.org/our-funds/#blm

> "The Movement for Black Lives, born out of the uprising in Ferguson, MO, has become a powerful, dynamic constellation of leaders and groups that have come together to tackle a variety of interconnected problems. The individuals of this movement are young, Black, queer, trans, feminist, immigrant, and undocumented leaders who are embracing grassroots organizing as a core strategy to educate and mobilize people to address state violence and injustice in Black communities."

This is how I found the Movement for Black Lives. No breaking news story, no 20/20 exposé. Just a quick mention in an article about another group and $100 million. You do not see their representatives on TV, they do not write op-eds, and no one in the media mentions them. Yet, they wield tremendous power in the movement. Before I explain the details of the Movement for Black Lives, I need to explain the rest of the funding maze I found.

Most people think of nonprofits as organizations like the ones in the examples above. They have tax-exempt status; they raise money and use it for their cause. That is the traditional way, but the industry has adapted due to the volume of charities and IRS changes. Large numbers of requests can inundate the IRS, creating a backlog. Also, with the advent of political PACs and other organizations that are nonprofit but do not qualify for tax-exempt status, the process has grown more complicated. Because of the time and cost associated with gaining 501(c)(3) status, many organizations needed help.

For example, let us say a family has a child with a rare disease and wants to start a charity to bring awareness to the issue and raise money for research. This is a worthy cause, but the family would likely not have the time or money necessary to draft the organizational paperwork, ensure they meet the requirements for 501(c)(3) status, hire an attorney, file the application, and so on. This is where fiscal sponsors can help.

A fiscal sponsor is a nonprofit organization that provides fiduciary oversight, financial management, and other administrative services to other nonprofits.[67] This offers a way for a nonprofit, often newly formed, to attract donors even when it is not yet recognized as a tax-exempt organization. Charitable contributions are given to the fiscal sponsor, which then grants them to support the cause. This is a normal practice and can be beneficial to a small nonprofit.

Opponents are incorrect when they say that Black Lives Matter is not a nonprofit. They are not operating with the purpose of making a profit, so they are a nonprofit, technically. If you go to the website and click on "donate," you will see the disclaimer, "Your contribution will benefit Black Lives Matter Support Fund at Tides Foundation." Next, under contribution rules it states, "ActBlue Charities is a registered charitable organization formed to democratize charitable giving. A copy of our latest financial report may be obtained by emailing info@actblue.com or calling (617) 517-7600."

Many also saw ActBlue and thought it was the partisan organization that raises funds for Democrat candidates.

---

67 For a detailed explanation, see the National Council of Nonprofits website at: https://www.councilofnonprofits.org/tools-resources/fiscal-sponsorship-nonprofits

ActBlue Charities is a separate entity. It was formed by the people at ActBlue but is dedicated to charitable funds. The Tides Foundation is a decades-old, reputable charitable organization that focuses solely on left causes.

Black Lives Matter's sponsor used to be Thousand Currents until a controversial connection was discovered. Thousand Currents, originally called IDEX (International Development Exchange), "partners with grassroots groups and movements—led by women, youth, and Indigenous Peoples in the Global South—that are creating lasting solutions to our shared global challenges." Susan Rosenberg is listed as vice chair on the Thousand Currents board of directors.[68] This partnership linked Black Lives Matter directly with a convicted terrorist.

Rosenberg was a member of both the Weather Underground, along with Obama mentor Bill Ayers, and the May 19th Communist Organization—an organization whose admitted purpose was to overthrow the government. After assisting in armored truck robberies and the bombing of government buildings, she was eventually caught in 1984 in possession of a large cache of explosives and firearms. She was sentenced to fifty-eight years in prison, but her sentence was commuted by Bill Clinton on his last day in office. Though it is no longer listed as a fiscal sponsor, Thousand Currents still mentions its association with Black Lives Matter on its website.[69]

---

[68] Thousand Currents' IRS Form 990 for 2017 lists Rosenberg as their vice chair in Part VII. It can be viewed online at https://projects.propublica.org/nonprofits/organizations/770071852/201901359349307325/full

[69] See: https://thousandcurrents.org/?s=Black+Lives+Matter

In addition to having fiscal sponsors, Black Lives Matter, Movement for Black Lives, and other groups also use intermediaries. A philanthropic intermediary is a mission-driven organization that aims to link donors (individuals, foundations, and corporations) with organizations and individuals delivering charitable services. Again, this is a great creation. It helps match donors and charities who may not have otherwise met.

There is nothing wrong with using these useful and beneficial methods to raise money. What is odd is the number of fiscal sponsors and intermediaries being used by the movement. Black Lives Matter is fiscally sponsored by The Tides Foundation (and perhaps still Thousand Currents). The Ford Foundation (sponsor) and Borealis Philanthropy (intermediary) founded the BLMF, a fund held for the Movement for Black Lives. The Movement for Black Lives (charity with no tax-exempt status) is fiscally sponsored by the Alliance for Global Justice (sponsor). Movement for Black Lives then acts as a sponsor, through its intermediary (and sponsor), to a host of other organizations, including Black Lives Matter.

It would be so much simpler to have one or two organizations with chapters throughout the country. It would result in easier fundraising and better messaging. But the Black Lives Matter movement is a complicated web of connected groups. It is basically a race-based Ponzi scheme. Here is a chart created by the Capital Research Center highlighting the organizational structure of the movement, as well as some of its funding connections.[70]

---

[70] Robert Stilson, "The organizational structure of Black Lives Matter," Capital Research Center, June 18, 2020. https://capitalresearch.org/article/the-organizational-structure-of-black-lives-matter/

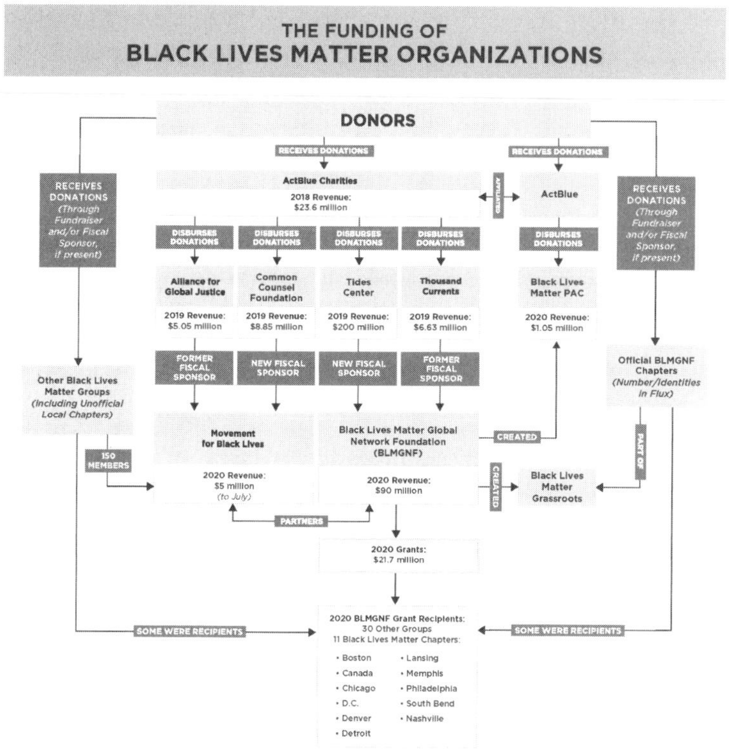

Capital Research Center[71]

Many of these organizations do not have websites, or they have pages with no information other than a way to donate. This makes it next to impossible to find out who is involved, what they do, and where the money goes.

---

[71] Robert Stilson, "The Organizational Restructuring of Black Lives Matter: Movement for Black Lives," Capital Research Center, April 29, 2021. https://capitalresearch.org/article/the-organizational-restructuring-of-black-lives-matter-movement-for-black-lives/

The most interesting thing about Black Lives Matter is not their IRS status; it is the fact that there is no longer a Black Lives Matter organization. They maintain a page and the means to accept donations, and that is really all that remains of the original organization. Black Lives Matter is largely controlled by the Movement for Black Lives and Black Lives Matter Global Foundation.

For several months, the country has been beset by protests and riots. It is obvious that they are organized, but many believe they are being funded by the Black Lives Matter movement or others with political interests. There is no doubt that funds are being used to fuel the protests, agitate against the police, and support rioting and looting. That people dealing with the uncertainty of employment during the COVID-19 crisis would use their limited savings to travel around the country to protest, risk arrest, and meet the subsequent cash bail, merely in order to throw a rock at a police officer, is as likely as a spontaneous uprising in Benghazi.

The question is: Who is funding these protests, particularly the clashes with police? After being attacked by the Republican National Convention protestors, Kentucky Senator Rand Paul called for an investigation to trace the corporations funding the protests and riots.[72] I agree with the sentiment, but I believe it will be nearly impossible to trace. There are so many organizations

---

72 Tim Hains, "Rand Paul: Someone has to trace the money flowing from corporations to protests, riots," *RealClearPolitics,* September 6, 2020. https://www.realclearpolitics.com/video/2020/09/06/rand_paul_on_bidenharris_really_in_a_civilized_world_we_have_people_making_an_argument_for_looting.html

within the movement, most of which have no financial declarations or lists of their members.

Consider a corporation that gives a donation to Borealis, which gives some of the funds to the Movement for Black Lives, which gives money to the Black Visions Collective, which in turn gives funds to Reclaim the Block. Reclaim the Block gives funds to Good Kids, Mad City, and someone there gives cash to a teen to incite a riot or attack a cop. Even if authorities traced financials, social media communications, and cell phone records, I do not hold out much hope they would ever connect the funds to Reclaim the Block, let alone the corporation that made the initial contribution.

And even if Black Lives Matter activists are funding the riots, there is a good chance that no one at the donor level knows. The BLM movement has a decentralized, bottom-up structure. As I have pointed out, the movement is really a collection of many groups with a common enemy. If you are fighting racism, capitalism, immigration, or any gender issue, you are welcome. Similarly, there is no true leader. Each group operates independently of each other, and each group is made up of leaderless individuals.

In the *New York Times* article "BLM is Democracy in Action," Barbara Ransby went in search of the reason this movement has not produced a Rev. Dr. Martin Luther King Jr. or Malcolm X. What she found is that it was by choice. Movement for Black Lives leads a coalition of groups that includes Black Lives Matter. The point is to allow each group and local organizer to make decisions.

Ransby writes: "The lead organizers of the Movement for Black Lives have been influenced by 40 years of work by black feminist and L.G.B.T. scholars and activists. Their writings and practice emphasize collective models of leadership instead of hierarchical ones, center on society's most marginalized people and focus on how multiple systems of oppression intersect and reinforce one another."[73]

The movement's organizational structure is both its strength and its weakness. Its strength lies in its ability to move quickly without waiting for instructions from "leaders." These local, social media-directed actions have been largely effective. Its weakness is the inability to control messaging or prevent crimes from being done in their name. If a Black Lives Matter Chicago member goes off script, you cannot call him into the office and fire him. You can try to separate yourself from the behavior, yet that is hard when they are wearing your T-shirts and using your hashtag.

The other thing that stands out in the article is the participants' belief that the male-centered model of leadership is a dead end. This sounds a lot like the messaging we saw on the Black Lives Matter website. There seems to be a strong focus on female leaders throughout the movement. It is also reflected in the organizations they support.

My point is not to indict these groups for their funding. Even if it is all aboveboard, it doesn't change the fact that under the guise of "racial equality," there has been a massive, intentional plot to reshape the country, it is happening right under our noses, and few Americans know the truth about it.

Now it is time to analyze the Movement for Black Lives in depth. There are many organizations in the movement, but you

---

[73] Barbara Ransby, "Black Lives Matter is democracy in action," *New York Times*, October 21, 2017. https://www.nytimes.com/2017/10/21/opinion/sunday/black-lives-matter-leadership.html

will quickly see why this is the most important one. While their anonymity is intriguing, their beliefs are dangerous. What they describe on their website is nothing short of an operational plan for the takeover of the country. You may not hear their ideas directly from them, but they have an army of surrogates and volunteers ready to espouse their talking points on their behalf.

To their credit, Movement for Black Lives is the only organization I could find within the movement to have a clearly outlined, detailed list of issues they'd like to address, demands for change, and suggested solutions to foster that change. They even include proposed legislation. In other words, they *are* the Black Lives Matter movement. Here is how the organization describes itself:

> "The Movement for Black Lives (M4BL) formed in December of 2014, was created as a space for Black organizations across the country to debate and discuss the current political conditions, develop shared assessments of what political interventions were necessary in order to achieve key policy, cultural and political wins, convene organizational leadership in order to debate and co-create a shared movement wide strategy. Under the fundamental idea that we can achieve more together than we can separately."

The next few chapters will provide great insight into the mindset of those providing organizational leadership to the movement. Note that, regardless of the constant use of terms like *black*, *trans*, and *war*, this is a political movement. Their goal is political power, and not from a dated Democrat or Republican mindset. They may seem aligned with the Democrats, but they hate both parties. They are simply using them to advance their goal. Democrats and Independents should take note of who they tell us they are.

5

Who We Are

In August 2016, the Movement for Black Lives (M4BL) launched the Vision for Black Lives—a comprehensive and visionary policy agenda for the post-Ferguson black liberation movement. The Vision, endorsed by over fifty black-led organizations in the M4BL ecosystem and hundreds of allied organizations and individuals, has since inspired campaigns across the country to achieve its goals.

The website is exhaustive in its information, and this is how we are introduced to the Movement for Black Lives. When someone calls out an extreme argument they have made, proponents will accuse them of making baseless attacks, taking the argument out of context, or racism. Often, they hide behind the bottom-up structure and say that a random supporter does not speak for the entire organization. To combat that defense, I will use their own words, directly from the site, and follow the quotes with analysis. We will start with how they describe themselves under the caption "Who We Are."

Right from the start, they put an end to the debate about what "defund the police" means. I have tried to explain to people that defunding police was not the goal, but rather a step in the direction they want to go. Their beliefs are italicized below:

> *WE ARE ABOLITIONISTS:*
>
> *We believe that prisons, police and all other institutions that inflict violence on Black people must be abolished and replaced by institutions that value and affirm the flourishing of Black lives.*

"We are abolitionists!" That immediately turns the "reallocate resources" argument on its head. Now that we understand what they want, we can focus on what it means. Obviously, it would mean an end to police shootings; but it would also mean the end of the organization tasked to quell crime and remove violent perpetrators from society, and thus, the end of civilized society.

In addition to abolishing police, they want to abolish prisons, releasing many violent criminals into society, most of whom will return to the black communities the activists claim to want to protect. They claim they will replace prisons, but with what? We are told that the new institutions will "value and affirm the flourishing of black lives." It is unclear what this means, but I'm sure it will do little to suppress the violent nature of the recently released criminal. And it gives no indication what will be done with prisoners who aren't black, a group that represents the majority of prisoners in the U.S.

> *We believe in centering the experiences and leadership of the most marginalized Black people, including but not limited to those who are trans and queer, women and femmes, currently and formerly incarcerated, immigrants, disabled, working class, and poor.*

Here is where their Marxist ideals are on full display. This is basically "black proletariat unite!" They add a 2020 spin which somehow always leads to an LGBTQ focus. It seems the movement cannot address any problem without mentioning trans, queer, women, or some other gender focus, yet they continue to ignore black men. To be sure, helping marginalized people is a noble act, and learning from their experiences can be beneficial, but it seems unlikely they can fix social problems by relying on leadership from "the most marginalized black people."

> *We believe in transformation and a radical realignment of power: The current systems we live inside of need to be radically transformed, which includes a realignment of global power. We are creating a proactive, movement-based vision instead of a reactionary one.*

This highlights another glaring chasm between their stated beliefs and what their supporters think they want. Supporters believe they just want to implement improvements. It is unclear what this statement means, but a radical realignment cannot be good. Radical, realign, transform; these are terms that imply a complete overhaul, and they were each repeated in this short statement for emphasis.

As for the transformation, we are never told what we are being transformed into. This sounds like the "hope and change" Obama promised, but we know that all change is not good. Also, this realignment includes a shift in global power. Here, they are openly stating their desire for America to cease being a global power. (This does not necessarily mean they want another country to lead, as they likely agree with the new "one world" nonsense coming from the left.)

> *WE BUILD KINSHIP WITH ONE ANOTHER:*
>
> *We draw from political lessons, grow in our leadership, and expanding our base to build a stronger movement.*

These statements are common in groups like these. They are empty words with no meaning, designed to exude positivity and make people feel good about the movement.

> *WE ARE ANTI-CAPITALIST:*
>
> *We believe and understand that Black people will never achieve liberation under the current global racialized capitalist system.*

Let us ignore for the moment the fact that capitalism has brought more people up from poverty than any other system. What are you for if you are an anti-capitalist? One would assume Marxism/socialism. If so, history tells us they are in for a rude awakening. If they were to achieve the Marxist system they are fighting for, they would find their blackness suppressed. One cannot be focused on blackness in an egalitarian system.

Racialized capitalism is a trendy new term amongst the black left. I will address it in greater detail in the section on The 1619 Project. Whatever they mean by this system, their reaction to it is an example of a strain of racism growing within black intellectual circles on the left. I call it the racism of self-inferiority. White supremacists say they are better than blacks because of their race, and blacks suffering from self-inferiority say that blacks simply cannot overcome the obstacles they face—although in most cases, the individual espousing the claim has achieved success himself. Their own example reveals that liberation comes from within.

These are the three guiding principles that explain their core beliefs and set the foundation for the remainder of the website. The first one—abolition of law enforcement—is a dangerous proposal, coupled with a radical anti-male sentiment; the second, about "kinship," is gibberish; and the third principle, anti-capitalism, places government—the same government they claim oppresses blacks—above the individual.

OUR FIVE-YEAR PLAN

> *Our movement and Black communities are not currently in a position to set agendas to scale, control the institutions that affect our lives, or create mechanisms to mitigate harm. This assessment should not be interpreted as a failure of our social movements, but it does expose a critical gap. We have created a popular strategy to guide us through the next five years; it is rooted in transformative goals*

> *that can impact the millions of Black people looking for direction and leadership in this moment. Chiefly, Black governance and ultimately positioning our communities to set agendas sits at the heart of M4BL Project 2024: Black Power Rising.*

This five-year plan communicates their strategy to achieve their goal of black governance and control of the institutions that affect black life. These institutions and levels of government are not solely for the black community, and it is unclear if their goal is to create separate, black-only institutions or simply take over the existing institutions. The latter would obviously be as racist as they claim the institutions currently are. Perhaps more racist since it would be explicitly for blacks. Here is how they describe it:

The plan comprises of five pillars: Mass Engagement, Local Power, Building Across Movements/Multiracial Strategy, Leadership Development, and Electoral Strategy. These five organizational pillars have "each with their own constituency of Black governance and organizational partners, drive each of our Black Power Rising 2024 goals."

> ***Mass Engagement***
>
> *We will engage 10 percent of (4 million) Black people within the United States, by providing political education, trainings, and cultural events. In addition, we will encourage and support individuals to engage in small-scale organizing in their communities.*

We will launch a number of distinct efforts and deliver regular, carefully crafted content to our folks in meaningful and innovative ways.

They seek to provide political education to ten percent of the black population. What they do not tell us is the nature of this education. From what we know of their beliefs, this political education will be heavy on anti-American sentiment and socialist propaganda.

Local Power

We will establish self-determined Black communities where Black people are in governing power in at least 5–10 localities over the next five years.

We must have the ability to create, shape, and influence agendas, and use state power and governmental resources to advance this agenda. We will engage in experimentation and clearly demonstrate what our vision looks like in practice.

We will create and operate spaces that serve as innovation hubs to deepen our base building, electoral organizing, and mass engagement strategies.

Sadly, many of the least successful and most dangerous communities for blacks are those where black people are in governing power, such as major urban areas. It seems evident that the best opportunities for blacks lie in communities where the residents are protected, bad behavior is discouraged, and the members of the community support each other, regardless of race.

However, they do not mean communities led by blacks per se; they mean communities led by the *right* blacks. As Rep. Ayanna Pressley said during a liberal Netroots Nation conference, "We don't need any more black faces that don't want to be a black voice."[74] When they talk about influencing agendas, they mean electing more politicians who espouse the types of policies most Americans would be against.

Building Across Movements/ Multiracial Strategy

We will align the left across issues, sectors, and identity, with a particular desire to maintain an intersectional analysis that elevates and centers anti-Black racism.

At a moment when the left is realigning, we will exert the logic, strategy, and vision of our movement as a leading force.

We will work across communities and reach outside the organizer class to build and engage majorities ready to organize, resist, vote, and build alternatives.

[74] Rebecca Klar, "Democrats don't need 'any more black faces that don't want to be a black voice,'" *The Hill*, July 14, 2019. https://thehill.com/homenews/house/453007-pressley-democrats-need-any-more-black-voices-that-dont-want-to-be-a-black

This is the most transparent and revealing of their political posts. They state they will align with the "left" and, once complete, exert the vision of the movement. For years, blacks have been saying that both parties take them for granted, and it is imperative that both parties are forced to earn the black vote. Here is an organization with a supposed black focus, openly saying they will communicate only with the left. By contrast, people who are solely concerned with uplifting the black community would never align with a political ideology. They would take solutions and assistance from anyone willing to engage.

> ***Leadership Development***
>
> *We will train 50,000 Black organizers, activists, strategists, and people in other essential roles to accomplish our five-year strategy.*
>
> *We will engage people outside of our orbit who are regularly in relationship with large numbers of Black folks, such as social-service providers.*
>
> *We will align preexisting leadership development infrastructures on the frontlines and support capacity building among local organizations.*

It would be interesting to know how they define engaging social service providers. Based on the tactics we have seen, it likely involves bullying and threats. However, they engage, what is most important is what they want these social service providers to do, but they have yet to tell us. Most of these workers are simply frontline employees for charities or the government. This is something to monitor.

Electoral Strategy

> *We will engage a strategy that captures clear electoral victories with an eye toward preventing the rise of white-nationalist and authoritarian rule.*
>
> *We will recruit and train civic engagement and advocacy strategists; challenge the existence of the electoral college; and drive advocacy to elevate local races that center our wellbeing and prosperity.*

Preventing the rise of white nationalists is a scare tactic used to motivate a specific demographic. White nationalists are not preventing blacks from doing anything, and whatever its alleged rise may be, no "electoral victories" are going to stop it. In fact, if there is an underground movement of whites bothered by the growing minority population or minorities in power, one could argue that blacks capturing electoral victories would embolden white nationalists, not prevent them.

Including "authoritarian rule" exemplifies their lack of understanding of the definition. If the COVID-19 crisis taught us nothing else, it taught us who the true authoritarians are. Not just lockdowns but selective application of the extreme mandates became the order of the day. Walmart may open, but smaller stores must close; draw "black unborn lives matter" on a sidewalk with chalk, get arrested, but paint "black lives matter" on a street in NYC, and the mayor will grab a paint roller to help. Go to church, get fined; loot and riot, politicians join you. It is as if government officials are using Saul Alinsky's *Rules for Radicals* as an instruction manual.

I am never surprised by anything the left does, but I have to say I am impressed. With all this focus on race and protesting, they found time to attack the electoral college. This is one of the most important mechanisms protecting our republic, which is one of the reasons the left wants to dismantle it. Without the electoral college, the left would have unbridled power, as the most populous cities are leftist bastions and would dominate the popular vote, controlling the "flyover country" they despise and do not understand.

The five-year plan reads like a political push for one-party rule. They openly talk about realigning the left. They ignore the fact that many blacks have reached tremendous levels of success in our system. It would make more sense to try to help others do the same rather than attempting to tear down the system that has helped so many. But it is obvious the movement has crossed the Rubicon, so onward they press. They have put their beliefs into action, laying out a plan for a new America: an America derived from the hearts and minds of anti-capitalists hellbent on abolishing police and prisons.

6

Preamble

The Vision for Black Lives section is the most important part of the website. It is where they lay the groundwork for the transformed America they desire. Unfortunately, the transformation is based on bias and guided by immutable traits.

It is appropriate that it has a preamble since it reads like a constitution. The preamble is the summary of their vision, an expansion of the "who we are" section, and a prelude to the 2020 platform. Perhaps more than any other section of the site, the preamble is a must-read for compassionate Americans who think this movement is harmless, let alone a net good.

The preamble begins with an acknowledgment that states, in part:

> The Vision for Black Lives is a collaboratively sourced document drawing on the wisdom of the Movement for Black Lives' ecosystem of

> over 170 Black-led organizations. We are deeply grateful to each of the authors and contributors to these policy briefs, to the members of the M4BL Policy Table who reviewed them, and to the external experts who contributed their time and brilliance to perfecting them. We want to specifically acknowledge and express our deepest gratitude, respect, and appreciation to the Harriet Tubman Collective, Black Women's Blueprint, and many individual Black feminists and Black trans women for calling us into more deeply integrating a Black queer and trans feminist lens and a disability justice analysis throughout the Vision.

There are two key takeaways from this acknowledgment. The first is that there are now over 170 organizations in the Movement for Black Lives' "ecosystem." The second is the group conspicuously missing from their focus—black men. They go on to thank those who helped them focus on black women, feminists, trans women, queer, trans feminists, and disability justice. For a movement that was started because black men were allegedly being indiscriminately killed by police, it is glaring that they did not make the list of focus groups.

> Black life and dignity require Black political will and power. Despite constant exploitation and perpetual oppression, Black people have bravely and brilliantly been a driving force pushing toward collective liberation. In recent years, we have taken to the streets, launched

> massive campaigns, and impacted elections, but our elected leaders have failed to address the legitimate demands of our Movement. We can no longer wait.

Here they seem to be blackmailing politicians: either meet our demands, or unrest will continue.

> In response to the sustained and increasingly visible violence against Black communities in the U.S. and globally, a collective of more than 50 organizations representing thousands of Black people from across the country came together in 2015 with renewed energy and purpose to articulate a common vision and agenda. We are a collective that centers, and is led by and rooted in, Black communities. And we recognize our shared struggle with all oppressed people: collective liberation will be a product of all of our work.

Where is this increased visible violence against black communities, and who is responsible for it? It can be argued that there is sustained violence being perpetrated on the black community, but it is not being done by the state, as the movement claims. The violence is being committed by people who live in the community. Too many are silent to these actions, and our government has allowed the violence to fester. It is a detriment to hard-working blacks and those who are successful to paint the entire community as oppressed people.

> We are intentional about amplifying the particular experiences of racial, economic, and gender-based state and interpersonal violence that Black women, queer, trans, gender nonconforming, intersex, and disabled people face. Cisheteropatriarchy and ableism are central and instrumental to anti-Blackness and racial capitalism, and have been internalized within our communities and movements.

It is true that they amplify these things; unfortunately, they also misidentify them. This is much like the misleading rhetoric on police shootings. We know the supposed epidemic is exaggerated; so is this claim of state violence. The groups mentioned obviously experience violence, but it is due to evil people, not the government. Also, many other groups of people also experience violence, but they are not mentioned because they do not fit the narrative.

They go on to create straw men to fight. Cisheteropatriarchy and ableism are made-up battles for the movement to fight, and I am sure if they are a problem, they are not "central and instrumental" to anti-blackness.

> There can be no liberation for all Black people if we do not center and fight for members of our communities who are living at the intersections of multiple and mutually reinforcing structures of oppression.

Uh oh. Whenever I see "intersection," I assume a list of "identity" groups is coming....

> We believe in elevating the experiences and leadership of the most marginalized Black people, including, but not limited to, women, femmes, queer, trans, gender nonconforming, intersex, Muslim, disabled, D/deaf, and autistic people, people living with HIV, people who are criminalized, formerly and currently incarcerated, detained or institutionalized, migrants, including undocumented migrants, low and no-income, cash poor, and working class, homeless and precariously housed people, people who are dependent on criminalized substances, youth, and elders. It is our hope that by working together to create and amplify a shared agenda, we can continue to move towards a world in which the full humanity and dignity of all people is recognized.

There it is! The identity jackpot; this time the list has grown. Few can say they have been classified as criminalized, precariously housed, or cash poor. These are just groups created to widen the tent of the oppressed. Religion has joined the fray, but only Muslims. When leftist groups mention religion in a positive light, it is always Islam. Their hatred for Christianity is expected, but they also hold contempt for Jews. It is important not to overlook the fact that they are also elevating the experiences of undocumented migrants, most of whom are not black.

> We recognize that building toward this world requires us to make demands of a state which has consistently created conditions of violence,

> deprivation, and exclusion for Black people, and to enter into a new covenant with each other. We seek solutions to violence within our communities that do not lie in the violence of a state and institutions created to destroy us, but in self-governance and mutual commitment and responsibility to each other's safety and well being. We are committed to uprooting the ableism and cisheteropatriarchy we have internalized, and to transforming the conditions that drive sexual, gender-based, homophobic, transphobic, ableist, and other forms of violence in our communities.

A new covenant? This is religious speech, which is odd phrasing for irreligious people. It may seem presumptuous of me to call them irreligious, but the evidence is overwhelming. No group rooted in Judeo-Christian values would be so focused on differences, be against individualism, have such a strong focus on entitlement, or spend so much time elevating LGBTQ people. It is also a fallacy to say black people today have been put in a position by the state where they are deprived, excluded, and exposed to violence consistently.

> While this platform is focused on domestic policies, we know that cisheteropatriarchy, ableism, exploitative racial capitalism, imperialism, militarism, and white supremacy and nationalism are global structures. We move in solidarity with our international family against the ravages of global racial capitalism and anti-Black racism,

> human-made climate change, Islamophobia, war, and exploitation. We join with descendants of African people all over the world in an ongoing call and struggle for reparations for the historic and continuing harms of colonialism and slavery, including structural and systemic sexual and gender-based violence, and we recognize and honor the rights and struggle of our global Indigenous family for reparations, land, sovereignty, and self-determination.

This is the third time that they have used "cisheteropatriarchy," their made-up term to attack straight people. The "racial capitalism" they mentioned earlier has now become "exploitative" and is accompanied by imperialism, militarism, colonialism, and white nationalism. It seems that the Movement for Black Lives is claiming the capacity to address racial problems on a global level and tackle climate change, Islamophobia, and war, to boot. Sounds less like the Black Lives Matter demands, and more like the United Nations.

> Articulate and support the ambitions and work of Black people toward our collective liberation. We also seek to intervene in the current political climate and assert a clear vision, particularly for those who claim to be our allies, of the world we want them to help us create. We reject false solutions which place profit over people, and rely on surveillance, policing, punishment, and exile to address every form of harm, need, and conflict. We believe we can achieve complete abolition

> and reimagination of current systems. We are already dreaming and practicing the world we want to live in.

This is a rare moment of clarity. "Assert a clear vision…for those who claim to be our allies" means that since Democrats have been saying they are aligned with them, it is time they start acting like it. They want unspecified "solutions"; but the solutions cannot include any commonsense things like encouraging profits, surveillance of criminals, protecting communities with police, or punishing those who prey on others. The way to achieve "solutions" is to tear it all down and rebuild.

> Together, we demand an end to the wars against Black people. We demand repair for the harms that have been done to Black communities, in the form of reparations and targeted long-term investments. We demand economic justice. We demand defunding and dismantling of the systems and institutions that criminalize, control, and cage us. We demand divestment from ideologies, laws, policies, and practices that harm us, and investment in our communities and movements. We demand political power and community control over the institutions which govern our lives.

Demanding to end a war that does not exist makes you seem paranoid. There is simply no war on black people. If there is a war on blacks, who is fighting it? The corporations and government entities who often prioritize blacks? This is not rooted in logic.

Here they also demand reparations and make another call to defund police. It is evident they want a black utopia where only blacks, not all people, are immune from being harmed.

> *We demand nothing short of liberation.*

They don't define "liberation." But they demand it, and it is all or nothing; they will not compromise.

> We have come together now because we believe it is time to forge a new covenant. We are dreamers and doers. This document articulates our vision of a fundamentally different world. And it recognizes the need to fight for policies that address the immediate suffering of Black people. These policies, while less transformational, are necessary to address the current material conditions of our people, and will better equip us to win the world we demand and deserve. We recognize that not all of our collective needs and visions can be translated into policy, and we understand that policy change is one of many strategies necessary to move us towards the world we envision. The policy briefs linked to each demand provide roadmaps and incremental steps to get there, elevate the brave and transformative work our people are already engaged in, and build on some of the best thinking and dreaming in our history of struggle.

Another call for a new covenant. Blacks are suffering, so it is time for a different world. They believe their demands are just the beginning of their work. To transform the world into what they demand, they understand that policy changes are key. They believe they have the best thinkers and dreamers. Yet they do their work anonymously. Why, if they are proud of it? These thinkers should sign their names to their work and publicly debate their ideas.

> This agenda continues the legacy of our ancestors who pushed for reparations, Black self-determination, and community control, and propels new iterations of movements for reproductive justice, gender justice, disability justice, migrant justice, healing justice, transformative justice, and climate justice.

Black self-determination is something I can get behind. If they genuinely believed it, they would scrap their government-centric, dismantle-American-society approach and replace it with a program of personal empowerment, mentorship, and community investment. More focus on acquiring skills and education, less focus on race and gender. They would also move away from the assorted flavors of "social" justice: reproductive, gender, disability, migrant, healing, transformative, climate, and restorative justice. Justice, plain and simple, is great; justice with an adjective in front of it is not actual justice, but rationalized inequality.

> We offer this renewed vision in the historic Black tradition of call and response, of principled struggle, and in a continued commitment

> to deepen our analysis, broaden our visions, and respond to changing conditions. We will continue to update the vision and our roadmaps in an iterative process leading us toward our North Star, as our movements, and the conditions we struggle in, grow and evolve.

What? I assume they had a word quota they needed to fill. This seems like a long, convoluted way of saying they will update the vision as needed.

Now we move on to their 2020 platform. There are six primary demands in the platform: End the War on Black People, Reparations, Divest/Invest, Economic Justice, Community Control, and Political Power. For each issue, there is an explanation of the problem, a clear list of demands, and proposed actions to be taken.

The first of these demands is to end the war on black people. Under this demand, they address thirteen distinct issues, many of which they describe as a "war." Not long ago, the left attacked Republicans for classifying various progressive initiatives as "the war on…"; for example, the war on Christmas, the war on religion, the war on traditional family values, or the war on straight white men. But now the left regard it as somehow appropriate to describe every way the black community is treated as a "war on black people."

"End the war on black people" is the longest and most comprehensive of their demands. To minimize redundancy, I will not list every demand. Instead, I will highlight those that are most interesting, dangerous, or antithetical to their proclaimed goal. I will respond to the problems they describe and the demands they seek, but I will list their specific legislative proposals at the back of the book. These thirteen issues will be detailed over the next three chapters.

7

End the War on Black People: Communities, Youth, and Women

We demand an end to the criminalization, incarceration, and killing of our people. We call for not just individual accountability of officers after a murder, but entire police departments.

END THE WAR ON BLACK COMMUNITIES

The Problem

Policing, criminalization, and surveillance have increasingly become the primary and default responses to every conflict, harm, and need, including those flowing from systematic

> displacement and divestment from infrastructure and programs aimed at meeting basic needs in working class and low-income communities. The result has been mass surveillance, criminalization, incarceration, and police and state violence, a drastically decreased focus on violence prevention and intervention, and a shredded social safety net.
>
> Surveillance, policing, prosecution, and punishment increasingly represent a primary expenditure of public funds. The U.S. currently spends over $100 billion a year on policing and another $80 billion a year on jails and prisons. In some cities and counties, the police budget represents 40–60 percent of the overall budget, while a fraction of public funds are allocated toward meeting community needs such as basic infrastructure, education, housing, public health, public transportation, social safety net programs, and youth employment programs.
>
> This investment in punishment over prevention has not made us any safer to the contrary, it has contributed to skyrocketing levels of police killings, rapes and sexual assault, physical violence, harassment and criminalization in Black communities.

In their description of this problem, they lead with policing. Police work is often ugly, and arrest numbers in the black community are grim; this makes policing an easy scapegoat. But the conclusions they draw do not come from a logical analysis or an effort to find solutions. They say policing is the primary response to "every conflict, harm and need." I do not believe policing is a valid response to most needs, but what should the response to conflict and harm be? They act as if policing is not the response to violent conflict that most in the black community desire and expect. Yet in most cases, the police are being called by people from the community.

They also make the mistake of making two problems one. If the problems in the black community are caused by divestment, this was not caused by the police. The expectation that an officer, called to handle a violent crime or domestic dispute, is going to consider how displacement and divestment within the community may have contributed to the situation is ludicrous. The officer's sole concern is protecting the citizens from whatever immediate threat is being presented.

This is an important reason their movement fails. Because they see the police as the primary problem, this is where they focus their energy. While surveillance, criminalization, and incarcerations may need to be reformed, they are not the root cause of the problems. Disproportionate levels of crime are the cause of the incarceration rate, not the police. And we must remember that these crimes nearly always have black victims.

The drafters of the document ignore the problems that are endemic in the black community. They make no mention of violent crimes, property damage, gang activity, lack of moral guidance and parental accountability, or failed educational institutions. In their view, police make black communities less safe. Once the problem is misdiagnosed, there is no way to find a solution. It is like the black community is suffering from a gunshot wound, and the Movement for Black Lives is prescribing a round of chemotherapy.

Next, they list police budgeting information as if there is a sole correlation to the black community. The numbers they provide, assuming they are accurate, are general numbers and are not reflective of funds spent on specifically policing the black community. This distortion is used to imply a police state when, relative to the population, it is not an overwhelming number. There are 330 million people in America and fewer than one million officers. These budget numbers are presented with no context.

Finally, they label every police killing as a "murder" and espouse dubious data like "one in three black men will be arrested in their lifetime." Think about that: That is more than six million black men. This, like the claim of "skyrocketing police killings, rapes and sexual assault, and violence," is a baseless claim pulled from thin air.

The Demand

> Repeal and replacement of the '94 Crime Bill...
>
> Invest in quality, affordable, and accessible housing, homelessness prevention, quality public education from pre-K through university, living wage employment, universal, accessible, community-based health programs, including accessible, voluntary, non-coercive, harm reduction-based mental health and drug treatment programs.

> Uncoupling publicly funded programs from law enforcement mandates, including mandatory mental health, drug treatment, or abstinence. Uncouple health and emergency responses from law enforcement: medical and environmental emergency funds should not be funneled toward a police response.
>
> Elimination of the JAG, COPS, and DOD 1033 programs.
>
> Eliminate police presence in schools, housing, public transportation, shelters, and hospitals.
>
> Decriminalize drug, traffic, and poverty-related offenses.

Repealing the 1994 crime bill is not the main issue here; many of its own supporters acknowledge it was a flawed bill. The issue is what will replace it. What the Movement for Black Lives has outlined so far, and many of their other proposals, clearly shows deference to criminals over the safety of citizens. The lawyers and legislators can hash out how much time an offense should carry, and the important work of issuing the punishment consistently, but this is an anti-punishment, anti-incarceration movement. There is no doubt they want to repeal the crime bill, but I do not believe they want to replace it with anything that would promote public safety.

Many of these demands are typical naïve solutions the left like to offer. They think if you simply defund or abolish police departments, then use the funds saved for minimum wage increases, affordable housing programs, and mental health support, crime will go away overnight. They obviously do not understand that human nature is flawed. People will commit crimes no matter how strict or lenient the punishment is. What they are proposing lessens the discouragement of crime and reduces our ability to remove violent perpetrators from the community.

Next, they address surveillance. Most Americans agree there should be limits on surveillance of private communication, but they are talking about reducing surveillance in public spaces, where there is no expectation of privacy. When they say, "completely disconnect from law enforcement and surveillance," they must be under the impression that all people caught on camera are innocent. Their approach seems to assume that crime does not exist.

The arrest rate on shootings in NYC is just over 20 percent, this in a city with thousands of surveillance cameras.[75] This will only get worse without the cameras. When they say they want fewer police and they do not want cameras recording public spaces, they are really saying they do not want criminals apprehended.

---

[75] Craig McCarthy and Aaron Feis, "NYPD data: Only about 20 percent of NYC shootings ended in arrests this year," *New York Post*, September 6, 2020. https://nypost.com/2020/09/06/nypd-shooting-arrest-rate-barely-tops-20-percent-as-gunplay-surges/

END THE WAR ON BLACK YOUTH

The Problem

Young Black people are demonized and criminalized in ways that limit their life chances at every point from birth to adulthood. Black youth made up 35 percent of arrests of people under 18 in 2018. Black youth are still twice as likely to be arrested as white youth. Black women 18–19 are four times as likely to be arrested as white women of the same age. These disparities persist even as juvenile "crime" rates and arrests have fallen.

Once arrested, young Black people are less likely to be diverted from the system, more likely to be referred to a juvenile court, and are more likely to be processed through the system than their white peers.

In 2014, Black youth were 14 percent of the youth population nationally, but 52.5 percent of the youth transferred to adult court by juvenile court judges, the highest percentage of Black youth transferred in nearly thirty years of data collection.

These disparities increase at almost every step of the criminal punishment process, stealing the dignity of young Black people and forcing them

> onto lifelong pathways of criminalization and diminished opportunity. Once pushed into the criminal punishment system, Black youth face myriad collateral consequences that harm their future, their families, and their communities.

It is unfair to say a segment of the population is "criminalized" when they are committing crimes. I am open to reforms and believe every opportunity should be taken to prevent putting children in the system. The data shows that being part of the system, especially at a young age, increases the probability one will be incarcerated in the future. However, when violent crimes are committed, or a youth is a chronic offender, there are few options other than to put the child in an institution.

That said, providing stats without context is misleading. For instance, saying that black youth make up 35 percent of arrests of people under eighteen without mentioning the crimes they commit does not give a complete picture. Are black youth committing a higher percentage of violent crime than whites? This information would add some context but is not provided.

They admit that juvenile crime rates and arrests are falling but mention it as an aside. This is important as it shows a flaw in their racial argument. If there is a correlation between crimes and arrests, perhaps a focus on behavior is needed. As to the decrease in arrests, it is more drastic than they imply. According to the Prison Policy Initiative, "Since 2000, the number of youth in confinement has fallen by 60 percent, a trend that shows no sign of slowing down."[76]

They go on to point out the discrepancy in the percentage of black youth transferred to adult court. I do not think children should be tried as adults except in the most extreme cases. This may be an issue that deserves a review, but it should be due to the number of children transferred to adult court, not the racial makeup of the children. It would also be important to know how often this happens. If half of the children were being referred to adult court, I would say we have a crisis, but they do not provide the percentage; I assume that is because the percentage is relatively low.

The Demand

> We demand that policymakers address deprivation of resources to public schools and the state-sanctioned violence that stems from law enforcement presence, including ICE, and criminalization in schools by: Removing police, armed security, ICE, probation, and metal detectors and other surveillance equipment and practices from schools.
>
> Divesting funding from exclusionary discipline and school policing…
>
> Ending corporal punishment.

[76] Wendy Sawyer, "Youth confinement: The whole pie 2019," press release, Prison Policy Initiative, December 19, 2019. https://www.prisonpolicy.org/reports/youth2019.html

> Ending "stop and frisk" and "gang policing" programs and databases.
>
> End criminalization of youth through status offenses such as curfew, truancy, and runaway laws.
>
> End the practice of charging youth with misdemeanors and limit the ability to charge them with felonies.
>
> End the practice of charging and incarcerating children as adults.
>
> Ensure effective implementation of prohibitions on youth solitary confinement and incarceration in adult facilities.

They open with a demand to address public school resources. Here they take another break from their black focus to echo a left-wing talking point. Any honest person addressing education in urban areas will tell you that the funding allotted to the public schools is greater than the cost of the average private school in the area. If they were concerned about public school resources, they would be demanding the abolition of public sector unions, especially teachers' unions, and a complete revamp of the pension system. This is where the resources are going.

Much of the remainder of the demands address policing and what they deem as "criminalization of youth." The problem is their proposed solutions leave teachers and administrators with few ways to maintain order and protect children. They want to end student searches and the policing of gangs while simultaneously removing all security measures from the school. No police, armed security, metal detectors, or surveillance on campus. As long as they address "rampant racial disparities," they have no concern for the larger disciplinary and safety problems they create.

They also want to end gang databases and the sharing of data with police and ICE, and implement a ban on suspensions, expulsions, and arrests for all pre-K through twelfth-grade students. They believe that no one under twenty-three years of age should be incarcerated. If the tools that help keep weapons and criminal behavior out of the schools are banned, disciplinary actions are forbidden, and offenders cannot be arrested, what happens to the innocent kids who are simply trying to learn? These priorities are misguided, and our children will pay the price.

What is sad is that they say nothing about improving academic excellence or putting students in positions to be successful. They focus only on removing punitive policies that deal with bad behavior and preventive measures that are in place to protect the students, most of which were implemented as a reaction to past incidents. To the Movement for Black Lives, punishing bad behavior is racist.

END THE WAR ON BLACK WOMEN

The Problem

The war on Black women, girls, trans, intersex, and gender nonconforming people takes many forms, including state, community, interpersonal, economic, and reproductive racial gender-based violence. Each fuels, facilitates, and reinforces the others.

Black women in the U.S. face some of the highest rates of interpersonal and community violence, including family, interpersonal, homophobic and transphobic, and sexual violence, childhood sexual abuse, "corrective" rape of lesbians and gender nonconforming people, street harassment, and stalking, in the United States.

For instance, Black women experience some of the highest rates of domestic violence, including fatal violence, in the country, and the second highest rates of sexual violence in the U.S. after Native women. Black trans women and nonbinary people and Black disabled people report the highest levels of sexual violence among Black people.

Although frequently erased from conversations about racial profiling, police violence, criminalization, mass incarceration, and deportation,

Black women, girls, trans, and gender nonconforming people are central targets of all forms of state violence, including physical, sexual, and fatal violence by law enforcement agents, criminalization, and incarceration.

Additionally, Black women are denied access to income support programs through time limits, family caps, restrictions on migrants' access to benefits, and impossible conditions of compliance.

Access to abortion, affordable birth control, and gender affirming, culturally competent reproductive and maternal health care is increasingly limited in Black communities.

A long legacy of racial and gendered discrimination, which shapes how medical professionals treat Black women. Black women have also been subjected to a long history of family separation, dating back to slavery. In addition to the family separation inherent in theft from the continent and the Middle Passage, it is estimated that "more than half of all enslaved people in the Upper South were separated from a parent or child." The myths of Black motherhood developed to justify the unconscionable practice of selling children away from their mothers and the high rates of infant and maternal

> mortality caused by the conditions of slavery persist to this day.

With the organization's focus on women, largely to the detriment of men, there is no surprise that the "war on women" is one of the longest sections. Many of the issues described have little to do with racism. Interpersonal and community violence are bad but are being committed against black victims by other blacks, likely the same blacks the Movement for Black Lives is fighting to prevent police from incarcerating.

They revisit their favorite target by arguing that women are "central targets" of state violence. As is common with these accusations, there is little evidence presented. Given the percentage of one group's incarceration compared to another group's does not prove racial animus; only comparing the amount of crime committed by each group could do that. Yet they see the incarceration discrepancy alone as a smoking gun of racism.

Poverty is mentioned as an attack on women as if it is deliberate or gender-specific. I guess when Jesus said, "For ye have the poor always with you," he was speaking solely of black women. They deem denial of access based on legal guidelines intentionally harmful to black women. The most outrageous claim is that abortion is limited in black communities. Anyone looking at the abortion rates by race in America knows this is foolish.

There are many other things they mention, like caregiving, foster care, and immigration enforcement. I did not include them all, for brevity's sake. You will find that they continue their focus on the trans community, even adding a new distinction, AFAB (assigned female at birth). Lastly, they claim that family separation and mortality rates of infants and mothers are caused by the conditions of slavery which supposedly persist to this day. This is right out of the playbook of The 1619 Project.

The Demand

> Pass legislation decriminalizing offenses which disproportionately drive women, girls, trans, and gender nonconforming people into the criminal punishment system, detention, and deportation...
>
> Pass legislation mandating that police, prosecutors, and judges consider past history of domestic violence in decision-making around arrest, prosecution, and sentencing.
>
> Release all survivors of violence from jails, prisons, and detention centers.
>
> Transition to a just economy that centers the needs of people over profit.
>
> Eliminate exclusions from worker protections for domestic and agricultural workers, tipped workers, migrants, and participants in the "gig economy."
>
> Pass legislation ensuring equal pay for Black women.

> Pass legislation mandating a federal minimum wage of at least fifteen dollars per hour.
>
> Ensure full access to comprehensive sexual and reproductive health care, including gender affirming care for trans, intersex, and gender non-conforming people, and eliminate discriminatory barriers to health care for all people.
>
> Ensure safety and protection for abortion clinics, workers, and patients without increasing policing and criminalization of individuals accessing clinics and surrounding communities.
>
> Abolish "crisis pregnancy centers" and redistribute resources to reproductive justice initiatives.

The movement is so heavily women-centered that it has amassed a long list of demands here. I cannot address them all, so I will just make a few key points. First, they believe the key to ending the "war on women" is enacting Democrat policies. They demand a list of them, including an end to the "gig economy," putting "people over profit," equal pay for black women, universal healthcare, raising the federal minimum wage to fifteen dollars per hour, and bail reform.

They want to decriminalize offenses disproportionately committed by women. Among these, they include "poverty related offenses." Does that include theft and fraud? They also want all survivors of violence released from jails, prisons, and detention centers. Do they get released if the crime they are incarcerated for was not perpetrated on their abuser? Women, they say, should also be exempt from punishment for violating probation or parole. This is the typical "treat us equally but not the same" rhetoric we hear from the new feminist movement.

They want to ban crisis pregnancy centers, which give pregnant women alternatives to abortions; yet there are several demands, including five proposed pieces of legislation, that protect and expand abortion. They also claim that black women are being blocked from having abortions. Whatever you believe about abortion, the statistics do not support their argument that black women are being denied access.

They have a lot of proposed legislation nominally aimed at supporting women. You can read through the exhaustive list and see the proposals in the appendix. These demands and the proposed legislation may be well-intended, but many do not address any racial or gender disparities, while others would create a separate standard of rights and protections only for women. This is not something you would expect from people working to advance equality.

8

End the War on Black People: Gender, Health, Migrants, Jail, Death Penalty

END THE WAR ON BLACK TRANS, QUEER, GENDER NONCONFORMING AND INTERSEX PEOPLE

The Problem

White supremacy, racial capitalism, cisheteropatriarchy, homophobia, transphobia, and ableism intersect in the lives of Black queer, trans, gender nonconforming and intersex people, fueling state violence, family, domestic, interpersonal and community violence.

> Discrimination, harassment and violence against trans, queer, gender nonconforming and intersex people pervade virtually every institution and setting…
>
> The current political climate, in which federal, state and local governments have overtly allied with the Christian Right, is fueling a full-on assault on trans and queer people.
>
> Black queer, trans and gender nonconforming people experience widespread homelessness and housing insecurity due to pervasive discrimination and structural exclusion in public and private housing and shelters across the country.

For those who need evidence that black people are not the priority of the movement, I believe this illustrates it perfectly. It is shocking to see an entire category on trans, queer, and gender-nonconforming people. This is not to say that their rights and protections aren't important, but when measured against the group's name and proclaimed purpose, the movement has included the rights of trans, queer, and gender nonconforming people in every demand thus far, and saw the need to address it separately as well. No other targeted group gets this level of attention.

Look at the things they claim fuel violence on this statistically tiny demographic. While there is no surprise that they list white supremacy as a cause of violence, no one would rationally contend that lacking a disability or being heterosexual fuels violence. The argument against capitalism is just as unfounded. The other items may exist, but are simply not prevalent issues in the black community. Next, they attack the Christian right, claiming they are fueling assaults on trans and queer people, when in reality, trans people and groups like this are the aggressors, trying to force others to accept and comply with their lifestyle.

This is not the last time they will mention the "Christian Right," so it is important to address the label. There is no such thing as Christian Right, just as there is no alt-right. Conservatives are a group of people with certain ideals and a particular worldview. There are people who share some of their political views who are bad, wrong, and racist; the same holds for liberals, but they are not called "alt-left." The term "alt-right" is simply a way to tie bad people to a broader group because they share views on a couple of issues. By that logic, the media should be calling Antifa liberals, but they do not.

This same tactic is at play in the Christian Right label. Christians are defined by their monotheistic God, their faith in Jesus Christ as savior, and their adherence to the Word of the Bible. This is neither right nor left. Like the political alignments above, there are obviously bad Christians, as human nature is flawed; but agenda-driven people have presented the flaws as one-sided, and it is always the political right who are bad. Christians who believe the Bible in its entirety are bad right-wingers, but Christians who ignore or dismiss parts of the Bible are "enlightened." True Christians should be concerned about the latter.

They end by saying that gender-nonconforming people experience widespread homelessness due to "structural exclusion" from housing. It is safe to assume that this includes a women's shelter that does not admit a man who lives as a woman, because the women in the shelter are uncomfortable. What are they supposed to do? There is no simple solution, and their stance on this goes against their belief of a pure democracy. Shouldn't the desires of twenty women in a shelter outweigh that of one trans woman?

The Demand

> End profiling, criminalization, police, and prison violence against Black trans and gender nonconforming people.
>
> Affirm gender self-determination in all aspects of life from birth. All trans and intersex people's medical needs should be included in health coverage at no cost, including full free access to all forms of gender affirming and reproductive care.

This is an extreme leftist ideology that purports to seek protection for LGBTQ people but is really pushing a broader political agenda. If you have already demanded an end to the profiling and criminalizing of black people, then black trans and gender-nonconforming people are covered. What is "equitable education for trans people" and how does someone exercise "self-determination" to affirm his gender from birth? They also demand that all gender care be provided at no cost. This would force citizens opposed to gender reassignment surgery to pay for it.

> END THE WAR ON BLACK HEALTH AND BLACK DISABLED PEOPLE

The Problem

> Black people experience significant health disparities with respect to cancer, respiratory disease, stress-related conditions such as high blood pressure and heart disease, and HIV.

> In addition to nonexistent and inadequate coverage, structural segregation and discrimination have profound effects on access to health care. Communities of color experience high rates of hospital closures, understaffing, under-resourced and poorly maintained health care facilities, culturally incompetent physicians, unfair and unequal access to preventative screenings and treatment, as well as proximity to toxic industries and environmental hazards. Further exacerbating health disparities, there are significantly fewer health professionals of color to provide competent and culturally appropriate clinical services for people of color.
>
> Universal health care is more than Medicare for All.

Black healthcare is a serious problem, and improving the state of black health is critical. It is important to look at the issue in two parts: black health and black care. From the standpoint of health, they highlight the problem by showing the disparities in the respective conditions experienced by blacks and whites. The stats are true, but much of the variance is due to personal choices and lifestyle.

They also describe an issue with "culturally incompetent physicians" and a need for "culturally appropriate" care. I understand a physician's need to understand things certain religions or immigrant groups may not believe in, but this would not relate to black Americans. The "culturally appropriate" care is difficult to understand. It likely stems from a small but often-cited study published by the PNAS.[77]

The study, titled "Racial Bias in Pain Assessment and Treatment Recommendation, and False Beliefs about Biological Differences between Blacks and Whites," claims that 40 percent of first- and second-year medical students held false biological beliefs about black bodies. This is clearly shocking and disturbing, but we must consider that the participants were students, and there were only 222 people in the study. This is not indicative of the level of treatment most black patients receive.

If lack of culturally competent physicians is the problem, the only remedy is more black doctors. A large pool of new black doctors would be tremendous. I can only assume that in addition to a cultural understanding, they would need to be highly competent. This will take an adequate educational foundation; however, it seems unlikely, with their focus on social justice to the detriment of STEM training. Expecting a growth of black doctors from our failing public schools is like mandating that everyone purchase guacamole while ignoring a growing shortage of avocados.

As for black care, this is where other factors come into play. Much of the problem as they see it surrounds insurance. Obviously, they support universal healthcare, but in lieu of that, they want Medicaid expanded. This is more of an economic issue than a race issue. They explain that 20 percent of blacks are uninsured compared to 12 percent of whites. This is consistent

---

[77] Kelly M. Hoffman, Sophie Trawalter, Jordan R. Axt, and M. Norman Oliver, "Racial bias in pain assessment and treatment recommendation, and false beliefs about biological differences between blacks and whites," *Proceedings of the National Academy of Sciences 113* (16), April 19, 2016, 4296–4301. https://www.pnas.org/content/113/16/4296#sec-1

with income discrepancies. If the comparison were poor whites and poor blacks, the gap would close.

They also point out that public resources are limited or have been displaced. This is the closest they will come to a real "systemic" problem, albeit a local one. In most of the highly populated black areas, from Atlanta to Baltimore, from Chicago to D.C., black people represent a large percentage of the local politicians and administrators. Mayors, councilmen, school board members, county board commissioners, congressmen—these areas have had majority-black representation for decades. One can argue that there is an operational problem; it is just not fair to call it racism.

The Demand

> Any new insurance coverage proposal must provide full coverage to everyone (including individuals of all immigration statuses),
>
> Removal of geographic, physical and economic barriers to accessing care, enabling individuals to receive the care they need wherever they live through:
>
> Hormones and gender affirming treatment and procedures for people who are transgender or intersex. An end to medically unnecessary ("cosmetic" and "gender normalizing") surgeries on intersex infants and children.

Universal quality, accessible, and culturally competent childcare.

As flawed as their views are, they must be commended for their consistency. Here again they focus on gender-affirming treatment and including individuals of all immigration statuses. I do not understand how an organization that is fighting for a racial community they claim is marginalized, believes that giving illegal immigrants full access to public services will help their cause. Resources are limited, and demanding that resources the black community is lacking be given to others is antithetical to the stated focus of the movement.

END THE WAR ON BLACK MIGRANTS

The Problem

It is currently estimated that large areas of the Earth's equator will become uninhabitable and a significant percentage of global coral reefs will be dead within decades, prompting massive migrations from the region.

Additionally, the U.S. government has engaged in military actions and implemented foreign policies around the globe designed to destabilize democracies and promote U.S. political and economic interests.

Even as actions by the U.S. government, state, and private actors around the globe are driving

> migration to the U.S. by people fleeing the extreme violence and economic and environmental devastation they produce, only to be met by closed doors
>
> In Africa and parts of the Caribbean, U.S. institutions like evangelical churches spread false narratives around race, gender, and sexuality that criminalize and create volatile unlivable conditions for women and LGBTQ+ folks.
>
> The U.S. currently bars entry to people diagnosed with certain medical conditions, Individuals deemed to have committed acts deemed "crimes of moral turpitude," or who are simply found to have engaged in prostitution (regardless of whether or not they have ever been convicted of a crime) in the past 10 years are also barred from entry into the U.S.
>
> Additionally, many Black migrants are ineligible for any form of relief, including a green card, DACA, TPS, or citizenship, as a result of contact with the criminal punishment system....

It is important to understand what they are saying here. They are arguing that climate change and the U.S. military are displacing people in Africa. America then unfairly closes its borders to these migrants when they arrive at our shores. There are several problems with this, but let us assume it is true. They are essentially saying that the majority black leaders of the migrants' home countries are not smart enough to make policies beneficial to their citizens, and the U.S. government should regulate businesses in Africa.

They complain about foreign interests in Africa when America is exerting its influence, but they are either uneducated or willfully ignorant of the aggressive takeover of the continent by China.[78] They consider it a problem that there are restrictions to enter our country, clearly implying that countries, at least the U.S., should not have borders. They finish by condemning countries that criminalize LGBTQ people, but place the blame on evangelical churches.

The Demand

> We affirm that migration is a human right...
>
> Immigration and foreign policies that respect the human rights of migrants, and that eliminate and repair the harms caused by U.S. imperialism in the Global South...
>
> Elimination of restrictions on entry to the United States.
>
> An immediate end to all detention, deportations, Immigration and Custom Enforcement (ICE) raids, and private and public immigration detention centers.

---

[78] Andrew Malone, "How China's taking over Africa, and why the West should be VERY worried," *The Daily Mail*, July 18, 2008. https://www.dailymail.co.uk/news/article-1036105/How-Chinas-taking-Africa-West-VERY-worried.html

> Mandatory, free, and accessible legal representation for migrants in immigration court…
>
> Access to all public services…
>
> Ensure that migrants who have come into contact with the criminal legal system would no longer be subject to mandatory detention and deportation.

This, like proclaiming "We are abolitionists," could not be clearer. "Migration is a human right" *means* open borders. Eliminating and repairing harms means reparations, not for American Descendants of Slavery (ADOS), but for migrants, too. These demands basically repeat "open borders" several times, then demand reparations for the migrants to help their homeland, and free access to all public services while they are here. If you break the law and are a migrant, you must also be released. Based on these demands, black men who are in the criminal justice system should identify as migrants. They would finally get a mention by the movement.

> END TO ALL JAILS, PRISONS, AND IMMIGRATION DETENTION
>
> **The Problem**
>
> The rate at which the U.S. imprisons its people and the staggering percentage of incarcerated people who are Black and disabled reflect a deep historical legacy of criminalizing Black

and disabled people during slavery and in its aftermath as a means of controlling our bodies, labor, reproduction, and resistance.

Guards exercise complete control over imprisoned people's safety and access to basic necessities, and are able to withhold privileges to coerce sex. Additionally, in many prisons for women, male guards are allowed to watch and regularly sexually harass and assault women and transgender people when they are dressing, showering, or using the toilet. Women and transgender people also report groping and other sexual abuse by staff during pat frisks and searches.

For survivors who have been abused previously, this environment further exacerbates their trauma.

Additionally, conditions inside prisons and detention centers, including overcrowding, widespread pest infestations, mold, unsanitary conditions, expired, rotten, and low quality and low nutritional value food, intermittent and contaminated water supplies, and intermittent electricity pose significant health risks.

Some police and security forces, prisons, jails, and immigration detention facilities, and virtually all services inside prisons, including canteen, phone services, and commissary, have been

> privatized, placing incarcerated people at the mercy of corporations bent on profiting off of caged Black people.
>
> Communities suffering from high rates of imprisonment also frequently experience the consequences of destabilized neighborhoods and families...

They mention some legitimate issues here. They are concerned about the safety of inmates and want unsanitary and unsafe conditions addressed. Violence in prisons is also a real problem. Our system should be able to punish criminals without allowing them to be abused. These issues should be addressed, but they are not solely black issues. The fact that some inmates abuse each other is evidence that they are not fit to be back in society—a point that is lost on the "end prisons" crowd.

They oppose prison privatization, citing bad conditions as a reason not to privatize—as if the conditions in public prisons are like those in a country club. There are many studies out there highlighting the problems with private prisons. In most cases, the argument is that no one should be making a profit on incarceration. I understand the sentiment, but they are forgetting why the government, and many around the world, implemented this model. Whatever your thoughts on private prisons, public prisons would be far worse without them.

They correctly state that communities that suffer from high imprisonment rates must deal with destabilized neighborhoods. This reads as if the conclusion is to stop imprisoning people and the neighborhoods would flourish. But crime itself creates ripple effects, and lots of crime will lead to an abundance of community problems. There is no evidence that shows releasing violent offenders into communities would stabilize them, or for that matter, not locking up offenders that terrorize their own neighborhoods would somehow benefit law-abiding citizens.

The Demand

Retroactive elimination of sentences of life without parole (LWOP) and sentences that will result in death by incarceration.

Immediate release of all elders, people in comas, on life support, or in end of life care in prisons and jails.

Immediate release of all political prisoners.

An immediate end to prison slavery. All persons imprisoned in any place of detention under United States jurisdiction must be paid the prevailing wage in their state or territory for their labor.

Policies for housing imprisoned transgender people should be based on individualized assessments that presume housing is assigned according to gender identity (rather than legally assigned sex).

The voting rights of all confined citizens serving prison sentences, pretrial detainees, and so-called

> "ex-felons" must be counted. Representation is demanded. All voices count.

They have a list of prisoners they want released. Keep in mind, this is in addition to all migrants, domestic violence survivors, and people twenty-three and under. Here they add elders, the terminally ill, people with life sentences, and political prisoners. Which of them are "political prisoners" is never defined.

Other highlights include paying prisoners fifteen dollars per hour. Yes, it says "prevailing wage," but they have already established they want that to be fifteen dollars nationally. Most people do not believe murderers should be paid the same as working mothers.

They also demand that transgender people be housed based on their asserted "gender identity." This seems difficult just based on practicality. If prisons are failing at protecting their current inmates, how are they going to protect people who will be obvious targets? They end by demanding that people currently incarcerated, not just ex-felons, be allowed to vote.

> END THE DEATH PENALTY
>
> **The Problem**
>
> The death penalty is morally repugnant, and represents a form of "legal lynching," which has targeted Blacks and other people of color, disabled people, LGBTQ people, and low and no-income people throughout its history in the United States.
>
> The death penalty is randomly and arbitrarily sought by prosecutors, upwards of 95 percent of

> whom are white, who have the sole discretion to seek or not seek death.
>
> To date, more than 165 people and counting have been declared innocent of the crime for which they were sentenced to death, and a number of innocent people have been executed.

There are obviously varying views on the death penalty, but you cannot be a religious Jew or Christian and say that the death penalty is "morally repugnant." The Word is clear on this. In Genesis 9:6, God says, "Whoso sheddeth man's blood, by man shall his blood be shed: for in the image of God made he man."

You can argue for compassion, or say in our secular government you do not want the state carrying out the death penalty, but you cannot say that it is morally repugnant. It should also go without saying that getting it wrong is unacceptable, and the conditions of the crime that dictate when the death penalty is warranted must be consistent.

> **The Demand**
>
> The death penalty is and always has been a tool used to enforce racism, ableism, and gender and sexual conformity. Our policy goal is simply to abolish the death penalty.

Whatever your views on the death penalty are, saying it is racist, ableist, and a tool used to attack gender and sexual conformity must be near the top of the many illogical and disingenuous statements in this platform.

9

End the War on Black People: Drugs, Surveillance, Bail, Demilitarization, and Criminal History

END THE WAR ON DRUGS

The Problem

Throughout U.S. history, drug and prostitution-related laws have consistently been used to criminalize Black people and communities. Criminalization of marijuana and cocaine was achieved through the deployment of racist tropes depicting drug-crazed, sexually predatory, and superhumanly violent Black people…

Statements by U.S. government officials confirm that the "War on Drugs" declared in the 1970s was a cover for targeting Black communities...

Separately and together, drug and prostitution enforcement have driven systemic and widespread racial profiling, discriminatory enforcement, physical and sexual violence, extortion and abuse, gross sentencing disparities, and mass criminalization, incarceration, institutionalization, civil commitment, detention, deportation, and exclusion of Black people over the past 50 years.

The "War on Drugs" has also contributed to creating dangerous conditions for people who use drugs, including violence in illicit drug markets, increased overdose risk, vulnerability to sexual, physical, and other forms of violence at the hands of law enforcement officers, and denial of necessary medical treatment to people in custody, resulting in death or severe pain and suffering.

As marijuana is increasingly being decriminalized across the country, Black people with drug-related criminal convictions are being excluded from legal markets, while they continue to suffer the devastating harms and collateral consequences resulting from prior convictions, including years spent incarcerated or under criminal punishment system control for actions that are now legal.

Like the issue of prison safety, here is another issue with which I will likely have some agreement. I have always understood both sides of the argument as it relates to drug use. As a teen, I railed against the "war on drugs." This was not because I advocated their use; I simply saw no way to win the war and believed if we were not going to solve the problem, we were wasting the money.

At the same time, I believe recreational drug use is bad. We have had enough time and studies to know the effects on the body and its level of addiction. People claim that it increases the creativity of artists. I would argue that may be true, but it also kills some of them at a young age. This does not mean I condone criminalizing it. We certainly need to find a balance between policing and providing addiction assistance, but acting as if drug use does no harm is reckless.

Whatever the proper course of action, it is an extreme oversimplification to say the purpose of our country's drug laws is to criminalize black people. There is no evidence of this, although the Movement for Black Lives claim U.S. officials confirmed it. This is often linked to a comment cited by Dan Baum in a 2016 article he penned for *Harper's Magazine* entitled, "Legalize It All: How to Win the War on Drugs." In it, he writes that John Ehrlichman, domestic policy advisor to President Nixon, told him that the war on drugs was started to attack his two enemies, the anti-war left and black people.[79]

There is no record of this exchange. Even Baum admits that after making the explosive claim, "Ehrlichman just shrugged. Then he looked at his watch, handed me a signed copy of his steamy spy

[79] Dan Baum, "Legalize it all: How to win the war on drugs," *Harper's Magazine*, April 2016. https://harpers.org/archive/2016/04/legalize-it-all/

novel, *The Company*, and led me to the door." We cannot know if this was really said or, if it was, if it was true; but it does not matter, because even if true, it is not the only fact in evidence. That statement might describe Nixon's approach to drugs, not that of the whole of America, which is unmistakably more complicated.

The government has been grappling with drugs for over one hundred years. Prohibition started with alcohol but soon moved to end drug use. There were varied laws and new enforcement agencies from FDR through George H.W. Bush. Drug enforcement did reach a new level under President Nixon, but it was not all at his behest.

In 1971, newly elected New York Congressman Charles Rangel met with President Nixon and demanded he take more action to stop the flow of narcotics into urban neighborhoods. He wrote in his 2007 memoir, "[We] worked closely together on what was the beginning of our international war on drugs."[80] Over time, other members of the Congressional Black Caucus voted overwhelmingly for stricter drug laws.[81] This does not coincide with the argument that the drug war was an effort by racist whites to criminalize blacks.

The document's authors then connect the problems of drugs and prostitution, claiming they have been used to profile blacks, unfairly enforce the laws, and apply discriminatory sentences. There is no doubt that this has happened to some and there should not be a separate way to "police" blacks. I believe that

---

80 Brian Mann, "Profile: Charlie Rangel and the drug wars," WYNC News, August 17, 2013. https://www.wnyc.org/story/313060-profile-charles-rangel-and-drug-wars/

81 Arun Venugopal, "The shift in black views of the war on drugs," *All Things Considered*, NPR.org, August 16, 2013. https://www.npr.org/sections/codeswitch/2013/08/16/212620886/the-shift-in-black-views-of-the-war-on-drugs

the same crime with the same circumstances and prior criminal history should mandate equal sentencing, but we cannot be sure that all things are equal in every case.

I am bothered by the incarceration levels in the black community, but what offends me more is the racist implication that blacks cannot help themselves and must use drugs and sell sex. This is what I hear in the argument that drug and prostitution laws are used to aid mass incarceration of blacks. As if drug addiction and prostitution are genetic traits. Whatever the reason for the laws, we should be able to make them more equitable *and* address the behavior.

They claim that drug laws are forcing people into dangerous situations. Again, as if blacks are incapable of abstaining. Finally, they argue that blacks with drug offenses are being locked out of the legal marijuana business as they suffer from their prior convictions. From what I have seen, it is not just those with drug offenses; few blacks are getting licenses for pot dispensaries. This in areas where, again, the politicians look like them and have been re-elected over and over. If blacks cannot get dispensary licenses in places such as Chicago, do not blame the non-existent Republican Party.

The Demand

Full decriminalization of drug and prostitution-related offenses.

Repeal bars to entry into the U.S.

Full and comprehensive reparations to all people who have been adversely impacted by the drug war and enforcement of prostitution laws.

> Create mechanisms for people criminalized by the "War on Drugs" to be able to participate in legal drug markets where decriminalization has already taken place.
>
> Investment of savings from decriminalization to meet the needs identified by all people impacted by the drug and sex trades themselves, regardless of whether they have experienced specific harms....

Full decriminalization would include hard substances and trafficking, something most would think is extreme. They come back to open borders again, although I am not sure how removing bars to entry into the United States eases the war on drugs. Whatever your thoughts on drug crimes are, I do not believe most citizens would agree with the demand for participation in the legal drug market. One can believe you should be free without believing you have a right to a job in a given industry. Finally, how do you invest in people impacted by the drug and sex trades if they have not experienced "specific harms"?

> END THE SURVEILLANCE ON BLACK COMMUNITIES
>
> **The Problem**
>
> The Edward Snowden leaks in 2013 revealed a vast surveillance apparatus constructed by the FBI and NSA that collects information on everyone in the U.S. and abroad. While the web

> of surveillance impacts everyone, the harm to targeted groups, including Black, Latinx, Arab, Muslim and migrant communities, as well as poor, homeless or indigent individuals, disabled people, and anyone receiving government benefits or using public services, people involved in the sex trades and other criminalized economies, people who may be seeking self-managed abortion and other forms of health care, and activists who challenge state and corporate power is grossly disproportionate.
>
> Despite the reemergence of violent white nationalism as the nation's number one threat to domestic security, federal and local government surveillance continues to target Black communities.
>
> Over the past 10 years, social media monitoring has emerged as a major threat to Black activists and people organizing for racial justice, providing unprecedented power to law enforcement to monitor our movements and the people we represent.
>
> All of these surveillance practices disproportionately impact Black communities, including migrants.

It is true that Snowden exposed unconstitutional surveillance by the government. This has been widely forgiven because it was exponentially increased by the Obama administration. While this should be addressed, the authors had to take a leap to make it a black issue. They admit it affects everyone, then list every group except for whites and Jews when describing who is harmed.

In their effort to portray the black community as the target of surveillance, they mention the "reemergence of violent white nationalism." They claim that white nationalism is the number one threat to domestic security but do not back up the claim. FBI Director Christopher Wray is also cited as the source, but that is not what he said. Speaking at a congressional hearing, the director said, "The danger, I think, of white supremacists, violent extremism or another kind of extremism is of course significant."[82] He lists three things, yet they latch onto the point that focuses on whites.

White nationalism has been mentioned several times, so it is important to provide some clarity around it. In most of the references to white nationalism, it is equated to white supremacy. White supremacy is the belief that whites are genetically superior to other races. White nationalism, on the other hand, is the desire for a nation that is predominately white. Both are rooted in bigotry but there are two important points that need to be made. One is that the two aren't mutually exclusive. It is possible to be one and not the other. Secondly, being a white nationalist doesn't make one violent.

More importantly, there are many nationalists. People who want to put America first needn't be white nor xenophobic.

---

82 Marshall Cohen, "FBI director says white supremacy is a 'persistent, pervasive threat' to the US," CNN.com, April 4, 2019. https://www.cnn.com/2019/04/04/politics/fbi-director-wray-white-supremacy/index.html

There are also black nationalists, people who literally want to split the country up into regions whose residency would be determined by race. The belief itself is not a terrorist action and the same should go for white nationalists. Anyone acting in aggressive ways against the country, or any segment of the population, is a violent extremist. There really isn't a need for the other distinctions.

In any event, this section is supposed to be about surveillance and the mention of white nationalism is a red herring. That said, the surveillance Snowden revealed is different from what they are addressing as a problem here. Most of it is conducted on the street, on public transportation, or in other public places where there is no expectation of privacy. As for the concern of social media, people offer up so much of their information willingly that surveillance should be the least of their worries. Regardless, the writers offer little evidence that this disproportionately impacts the black community.

The Demands

> Transformation in the relationship between technology and the economy to prevent the expansion of surveillance capitalism.
>
> Moratoriums on the digital devices used to police race and poverty.
>
> Increased accountability of platform companies to Black communities.

> An end to the long-standing monitoring and criminalization of Black people.
>
> Elimination of gang databases and related information sharing, and opportunities for individuals placed on gang databases to receive notice and an opportunity to seek removal.
>
> Elimination of surveillance of targeted communities, including people accessing public benefits, hospitals, and services, disabled people, people in the sex trades, people seeking and providing information about self-managed abortion, political activists, Arab, Muslim, Middle Eastern, and South Asian people and communities, and people on probation or parole. Any policy solution should create the most room for abolition possible.

The authors have invented a new type of capitalism—"surveillance capitalism"—and they do not like it. I am not sure how they plan on transforming it. They demand a moratorium on the use of digital devices, but it is unclear by their statement if it is all device usage or just that which is used to police race and poverty. Ending the usage would hurt public safety; ending the usage solely on race and poverty would be confusing and ineffective.

To increase the accountability on social media platforms, people will have to stop signing away their rights, but again, I am unsure how this is to be implemented solely for black communities. The same goes for eliminating databases of criminals, which is what gang databases are, and of "targeted" groups. I am not sure how the list was selected, and I doubt that people seeking and providing information about self-managed abortions are high on the FBI watchlist. I believe it is the job of the probation and parole officers to monitor their assigned subjects.

> END TO PRETRIAL DETENTION AND MONEY BAIL
>
> **The Problem**
>
> The use of pretrial detention and money bail has contributed to the 500 percent explosion in U.S. jail and prison populations over the last forty years. Tonight around 600,000 people will sleep in a local jail. Over 75 percent, or about 462,000 people, have not been convicted of any crime...
>
> Many factors contribute to unequal bail outcomes for Black people including: judicial bias, where judges believe racial stereotypes that Black people are more dangerous; to centuries of economic discrimination and hardship that make it less likely for Black people be able to afford bail; to prosecutors trumping up charges for Black people.

I have been on the record for years saying few things bother me more, specifically related to the criminal justice system, than our inability to provide the speedy trial guaranteed in the Constitution. No one should get a trial date, be found guilty, then be told they are sentenced to time served because they sat in jail for months or years waiting for the trial. What if they were found innocent? This is a problem and needs to be addressed; however, the approach they take is misguided and extreme.

They want to end all bail. They accurately argue that it is intended to guarantee that people will show up, which is not always the case, but that is not the only problem. Some are repeat offenders or violent. They need to post bail or remain in jail until their trial, which should be set more quickly. The no-bail argument is flawed, and we can just look at New York City and Chicago to see the effects. Being a criminal does not make a person stupid, and if they know they will not be held for a crime, especially one deemed "non-violent," they will just continue to wreak havoc on the community.

The Demand

> End pretrial detention and money bail, electronic shackling, and unnecessary, burdensome, restrictive, and often impossible conditions as a condition of release from pretrial detention.
>
> Ensure that people have the support they need to return to court to fight the cases against them, including text reminders of court dates, transportation, and childcare support.
>
> Reduce racial disparities throughout the system.
>
> Enact comprehensive pretrial reforms including: speedy assessment and release within 24 hours; the right to a speedy trial; the right to counsel at first appearances

> Eliminate criminal and civil fees and fines, including costs imposed in connection with pretrial conditions of release.

Ending the pretrial bail for all is not the solution, and I do not see why sending them home with an electronic monitor would be an issue. It is not the government's job to find support—meaning taxpayer money—to ensure they return to court; that is why we have the bail. Just say the words "Reduce racial disparities" as a rationale, and everything proposed is supposed to be okay. I am onboard with speedy trials, but these authors are treating criminals better than law-abiding citizens. They want to eliminate criminal fees and civics fees in connection with courts, but the rest of us are buried by municipal fees every day.

> THE DEMILITARIZATION OF LAW ENFORCEMENT
>
> **The Problem**
>
> Since 1990, the U.S. Department of Defense (DoD) has transferred over $6 billion in military grade equipment to local police departments across the country, including campus and school police, under the Excess Property 1033 Grant program.
>
> There is little transparency regarding which police departments and campuses receive military equipment under the program...

The Demand

> We Demand an immediate end to transfer of military equipment to state and local law enforcement agencies, campus and school police, and medical facilities.
>
> Accountability for law enforcement agencies which deploy military weapons against Black people and communities.

They are demanding that the federal government stop giving state and local police forces—which they have already announced they want to abolish—specialized vehicles and tools, even if they are free. The reason is obvious: because these law-enforcement tools are intimidating and make it more difficult for criminals to loot, riot, and attack the police. Many of these tools are used to deescalate and minimize physical altercations. The authors claim there is little transparency on what the police departments receive, but that can be corrected without ending these transfers.

> END THE USE OF PAST CRIMINAL HISTORY
>
> **The Problem**
>
> Over the last 40 years, the reach of the criminal punishment system in the U.S. has expanded beyond contemporary and historical norms: there are currently 2.3 million people in state, federal, military, and Indian Country prisons,

> jails, and detention centers, civil commitment centers, and state psychiatric hospitals, and another five million on probation or parole.
>
> This population is disproportionately Black. Due to systemic anti-Black racism and profound racial disparities at every stage of the criminal punishment system...
>
> 42 percent of people arrested and booked three or more times were Black.
>
> **The Demand**
>
> Ban the Box: prohibit public and private employers from asking questions about criminal record history on employment applications until later in the decision-making process.
>
> Eliminate restrictions on voting, public assistance, professional licenses, housing, education, financial aid, parental rights, and adoption for people with prior criminal records. All people with prior convictions should regain these rights and privileges as well.

What they are really saying is that there are too many black people in jail, and a large percentage of them have multiple arrests. This, they imply, is not the fault of the individual and has nothing to do with criminality; it is the result of "anti-black racism."

This can easily be debunked. Ninety-five percent of blacks are not in the criminal justice system. If there were prevalent anti-black racism, that number would be far lower. And the majority of those who are in the system are in areas with large black populations. Wouldn't the blacks who live in majority-white areas be hated more and easier to find?

Regardless of how criminals ended up in the system, they are arguing here for ways to help them reintegrate into society. This is an important and necessary step in allowing them a second chance and reducing recidivism. Nonetheless, prohibiting employers from knowing the criminal history of their applicants is deceptive and not the answer. The key is matching the ex-felon with someone who will help him convince employers to hire him despite his record. For some jobs, however, employers must be able to consider the nature of the crime and, in some cases, to say no *because* of the conviction.

This concludes the first of six sections that comprise the demands within the Vision for Black Lives. The authors have not fleshed out the remaining five sections with this level of detail, but they plan to expand on them. Though incomplete by the exhaustive standards of the first demand, there is enough there to get a clear understanding of the issues they want to prioritize, as well as how they plan to address them.

10

Other Demands, Reparations, Divest/Invest, Economic Justice, Community Control, and Political Power

REPARATIONS

We demand reparations for past and continuing harms. The government, responsible corporations and other institutions that have profited off of the harm they have inflicted on Black people—from colonialism to slavery through food and housing redlining, mass incarceration, and surveillance—must repair the harm done. This includes:

> Reparations for the systemic denial of access to high quality educational opportunities in the form of full and free access for all Black people (including undocumented and currently and formerly incarcerated people) to lifetime education including: free access and open admissions to public community colleges and universities, technical education (technology, trade and agricultural), educational support programs, retroactive forgiveness of student loans, and support for lifetime learning programs.

Education is the most important issue affecting the future of black youth and is the best means to improve one's status in life. That said, it is appalling that not only is it such a low priority for those who claim to be seeking justice for blacks, but when it is mentioned, they attack the messenger, claiming they are missing the bigger issue of systemic racism. Just once, I would like them to appreciate the powerful position blacks are in and the tremendous strides that could be made if they shifted their focus.

In many urban centers, blacks hold a monopoly on the public education system, yet the activists are misdirecting their grievances. Even if the community got a cash windfall, it would be given to, or managed by, the same administrators and politicians to whom they have given a pass. Hold them accountable, demand better, and things will change. No reparations required.

> *Reparations for the continued divestment from, discrimination toward and exploitation of our communities in the form of a guaranteed minimum*

> *livable income for all Black people, with clearly articulated corporate regulations.*

Much of this was addressed in the previous point. I will only add that the extreme demands the newly woke whites and anti-racist blacks espouse are unconstitutional. Thousands of people fought for decades demanding equality, pushing to remove race as a determinant factor, only for "progressives" to set us back. For those who think this movement is good, consider this: In order to give the mob what they want, we would have to repeal the Civil Rights Act of 1964.

> *Reparations for the wealth extracted from our communities through environmental racism, slavery, food apartheid, housing discrimination and racialized capitalism in the form of corporate and government reparations focused on healing ongoing physical and mental trauma, and ensuring our access and control of food sources, housing and land.*

This seems like a junk drawer demand, just a collection of random grievances. "Environmental racism" is one of many invented academic terms that largely means nothing. Where there are discrepancies found, they tend to be economic, not racial. Slavery was evil but is not an issue in the black community today. Since slavery is the entire point of The 1619 Project, I will address the issue in detail in that section.

"Food apartheid" should be defined as a reason not to get a Ph.D. I am only half kidding. These people spend too much time creating shockingly debasing terms and not enough time thinking through their concepts. They are basically saying that black communities lack access to high-quality food, and it is due to racism. The real problem is a combination of poor eating habits and a "can't do" attitude. If you open a restaurant with quality food in these neighborhoods, people will go. Too many assume they will not, so they do not try.

Further, saying it is racist to open a fast-food restaurant in a black neighborhood is to not understand racism. And if the organic food is too expensive, again that is an economic issue, not "apartheid." Someone needs to explain to these academics that in apartheid and systemic racism, there are laws preventing a certain segment from doing things or living in places, not simply the hurdle of affording it.

> Reparations for the cultural and educational exploitation, erasure, and extraction of our communities in the form of mandated public school curriculums that critically examine the political, economic, and social impacts of colonialism and slavery, and funding to support, build, preserve, and restore cultural assets and sacred sites to ensure the recognition and honoring of our collective struggles and triumphs. Legislation at the federal and state level that requires the United States to acknowledge the lasting impacts of slavery, establish and execute a plan to address those impacts. This includes the immediate passage of H.R.40, the "Commission to Study Reparation Proposals for African-Americans Act."

The cultural histories of the slaves were indeed erased. This is abhorrent, but no amount of money will "repair" it, and the lives of the dead cannot be restored. For today's black public-school students, American *is* their culture. Learning the truth is good, as is a critical examination. What is damaging is an unhealthy focus on past wrongs with no context, or ignoring positives and twisting facts to imply that blacks are suffering from the effects of slavery today. As for H.R.40, I say, have the conversation and take the vote. If it is done honestly and not made up of members of this illogical movement, the results will be: Slavery was evil, it cannot be fixed, no one will be paid.

> **INVEST-DIVEST**
>
> We demand investments in the education, health and safety of Black people, instead of investments in the criminalizing, caging, and harming of Black people, a reallocation of funds at the federal, state and local level from policing and incarceration (JAG, COPS, VOCA) to long-term safety strategies, the retroactive decriminalization, immediate release and record expungement of all drug related offenses and prostitution, and reparations for the devastating impact of the "war on drugs"...
>
> Real, meaningful, and equitable universal health care, a divestment from industrial multinational use of fossil fuels and investment in community-based sustainable energy solutions, a cut in military expenditures and a reallocation of those funds to invest in domestic infrastructure and community well-being.

Either they were getting tired or they were not reading their own platform, because much of this is repetitive. Reallocate police funds, universal healthcare, and more money for education. They did add divesting from fossil fuels. Looks like they were near the end and wanted to make sure they included every leftist political talking point in their platform. For a supposed pro-black organization, they sound more like Bernie Sanders than Malcolm X.

ECONOMIC JUSTICE

> We demand economic justice for all and a reconstruction of the economy to ensure Black communities have collective ownership, not merely access. This includes: A progressive restructuring of tax codes at the local, state, and federal levels to ensure a radical and sustainable redistribution of wealth, Federal and state job programs that specifically target the most economically marginalized Black people, an end to the Trans-Pacific Partnership, and financial support of Black alternative institutions...

I have previously stated that adjectives in front of "justice" always negate the concept of justice, and this is no exception. The demand is basically the Black New Deal, or the Green New Deal with a black edge to it. There is a black focus on aid, grants, jobs, financial support, and interest-free loans. For progressives, it opens with a direct demand to redistribute wealth, though it lacks a formal "from whom to whom." This is followed by restoring the Glass-Steagall Act, Ending the Trans-Pacific Partnership, and organizing workers.

This will end in disappointment in the black community. I give them credit for at least mentioning blacks, but much of this will be deemed unconstitutional and the rest will be greatly weakened in its application. The problem is there is a lot of alleged giving but no foundation. At least the Green New Deal had provisions to identify jobs that will be in demand and develop skills specifically for those jobs. But this is just classic tax and spend. As my friend says, "Same soup, reheated."

COMMUNITY CONTROL

> We demand a world where those most impacted in our communities control the laws, institutions, and policies that are meant to serve us—from our schools to our local budgets, economies, police departments, and our land—while recognizing that the rights and histories of our Indigenous family must also be respected. This includes:
>
> An end to the privatization of education and real community control by parents, students and community members of schools including democratic school boards and community control of curriculum, hiring, firing and discipline policies.

If the previous two demands sounded like quotes from Joe Biden's website, this sounds like an old edict you would find in Karl Marx's writing. Demanding that those most impacted control everything, including the "land," is not just Marxist, it is stupid. The people most impacted by the police department are criminals. Should they control the criminal justice system? Besides, why do they keep attempting to sound rational? They have already told us they want to abolish the police; therefore, there is nothing for the criminals to control.

Here they demand an end to private school. This is a new one. I know they hate school choice, but that was supposed to be to keep the poor students in their failing neighborhood schools so the district does not lose its funding. This sounds like taking the option away from parents who can afford the tuition at the private school. I guess they want to maximize the number of students indoctrinated by their Marxist curriculum, and private schools are less likely to add it to their curriculum.

> **POLITICAL POWER**
>
> We demand independent Black political power and Black self-determination in all areas of society.
>
> An end to the criminalization of Black political activity including the immediate release of all political prisoners and an end to the repression of political parties.
>
> Election protection, electoral expansion and the right to vote for all people including: full access, guarantees, and protections of the right to vote for all people through universal voter registration, automatic voter registration,

> pre-registration for 16-year-olds, same day voter registration, voting day holidays, Online Voter Registration (OVR), enfranchisement of formerly and presently incarcerated people, local and state resident voting for undocumented people, and a ban on any disenfranchisement laws.

They do not want independent political power. They want more control within one party. If an independent black political party were created, I am sure all black voters would not be welcomed. There is no political activity, black or otherwise, that is being criminalized, and there are no political prisoners. They completed the circle by adding universal voter registrations, which to clarify means illegals can vote, and finally, by lowering the voting age to sixteen.

> **RESPECT PROTESTORS**
>
> We demand that the rights of protestors be respected and protected and that there be no abuse of powers. We Demand:
>
> Violations of property should never be equated with the violation of human life. That local and state officials ensure that there are no abuse of powers. No use of lethal force on protestors.

This is the first amendment to their twisted constitution. This is not one of their original demands; instead, it is the answer to their attacks on police and America. They can see that favorability of the protestors is shifting, and at some point, law enforcement will be allowed to do their jobs. In response to this, they demand that the police stop protecting property and allow people to riot and loot. Additionally, anyone who has been arrested must be released, as well.

This concludes the Movement for Black Lives 2020 Platform.

Here are some highlights:

While they want to abolish the police, whatever they claim to want to replace it with will be useless. They want to pass laws giving preference to specific groups of people, ultimately repealing the Civil Rights Act of 1964 and all the progress that came with it. They are anti-capitalists who want to redistribute wealth, yet they want to guarantee access to legal pot dispensaries for people with drug convictions. No one has a "right" to a particular industry, and pot dispensaries, legal or illegal, function under capitalism, so the movement should be against them.

They are aggressively pro-woman. In fact, they place a lot of their focus on people who are femme, queer, trans, disabled, Muslim, gender nonconforming, migrants, drug addicts, sex workers, formerly and currently incarcerated, and illegal, yet they never mention men or Jews. At least they removed the anti-Semitic language that used to be there, yet the attacks on Christians remain. As for men, the movement is supposedly about men being indiscriminately shot by police, but when you pull back the veil, there is no mention of this issue at all.

The Movement for Black Lives is a force, yet they have remained in the shadows. I hope you will do internet searches to see what comes up. You will find mentions, but you'll be surprised how few there are and how none are associated with any person. We at least know the faces of the women who started Black Lives Matter, though they are largely figureheads today. But we know nothing about the minds behind the Movement for Black Lives.

Someone must be in charge, or there must be some leadership group. The platform is too detailed, there is too much direction, too many groups, and too much money. Black Lives Matter may be decentralized, but someone understands that all this momentum means nothing if you cannot turn it into action, and that cannot happen from the bottom. There are forty million blacks in America, and we do not all agree. In addition, you cannot send forty million individual demands, and we cannot all be at the table.

It reminds me of Ayn Rand's novel *Atlas Shrugged*. There were whispers of someone named John Galt. The message was sprawled around town, "Who is John Galt?' For a while, it seemed like just a saying; no real person, just a rallying cry that exemplified a movement. But when it came to the secret hideaway, Galt's Gulch, someone made that happen, and someone was in charge. The same goes for the Movement for Black Lives.

Prior to this, people could claim ignorance. They would see the looters and rioters on TV and think, "Those are just a few bad actors; they shouldn't take away from Black Lives Matter's great message." That assumption can be forgiven, but it highlights the importance of this book. If you have made it this far and still think you can separate the good, what little there is, from the toxic, you are fooling yourself. I have made it abundantly clear that these groups are not focused on blacks; they are anti-American, heavily gender-focused, and have little, if anything, to do with police brutality. Corporations who donate to them are contributing to their own demise, blacks who march with them are marching for perpetually bad neighborhoods, and whites who support them are supporting their future unemployment. Do it at your own peril and the peril of the country.

If we can awaken the masses and have them push back against the radical demands of Black Lives Matter, it would be a small win, but we would still have an uphill battle against the progressive racism movement. Even without the intimidation of activists or the skewed policing data, they have an ace up their sleeve. What if they could guarantee the next generation is malleable to their twisted world view? They can, if we hand our children over to them. This brings us to The 1619 Project.

THE 1619 PROJECT

11

The 400-Year Lie

While the Black Lives Matter movement professes to be solely focused on police brutality, The 1619 Project also has a primary focus: slavery. This alone should cause people to scrutinize it more closely or dismiss it out of hand; instead, it draws them in closer, compelled like gawkers at a crash site.

The Project's argument is simple: Slavery is the cause of all the problems in black America; therefore, understanding and addressing this is the only cure for the disease. To understand how they got there, it is best to begin with the words of *New York Times Magazine* editor-in-chief, Jake Silverstein.

The Project starts with an introduction from Silverstein titled, "Why We Publish The 1619 Project." Here, he makes the argument that 1619 is not a year most Americans know, and he explains that this is when the first twenty or thirty enslaved Africans were brought to the English colony in Virginia. He then declares, "This is sometimes referred to as the country's original sin, but it is more than that: It is the country's very origin."

If slavery is viewed as America's origin rather than a permitted sin, The 1619 Project argues it would change everything about the history of the country. It would demand a new focus on past sins and force us to re-evaluate every perceived achievement through a different lens. Silverstein notes:

> Out of slavery—and the anti-black racism it required—grew nearly everything that has truly made America exceptional: its economic might, its industrial power, its electoral system, its diet and popular music, the inequities of its public health and education, its astonishing penchant for violence, its income inequality, the example it sets for the world as a land of freedom and equality, its slang, its legal system and the endemic racial fears and hatreds that continue to plague it to this day.

There is a lot to absorb in that statement, and I will address each point later when discussing the essays that follow. However, that statement summarized the foundation on which The 1619 Project is built. The logical question is to ask: Is it true? If it is true, one must wonder why no historians had discovered all these connections before. If it is not true, what is the purpose of making it up and creating such a tremendous marketing campaign behind a lie? I believe we will find the answer to this question within the collection of essays presented in the project.

As we go through various essays in The 1619 Project, an obvious theme emerges. They have long-held, deep-seated contempt for the country. Their version of American history has seared within them a clear memory of events that they never experienced. The essayists craft their tales like well-intentioned historians suffering from the Mandela Effect: the widespread belief that something has occurred, when it actually did not. This effort is purpose-driven, not fact-driven. The editor makes this clear in the Project's stated goal:

> The goal of The 1619 Project is to reframe American history by considering what it would mean to regard 1619 as our nation's birth year. Doing so requires us to place the consequences of slavery and the contributions of black Americans at the very center of the story we tell ourselves about who we are as a country.

The "why" is articulated clearly here: reframe American history and tell a new "story" about our country and ourselves. Placing the consequences of slavery at the center of the Project highlights what they believe is the biggest problem in America, and with all the focus shifted to that problem, we can better understand it and find a solution.

This would be great if they were correct. Unfortunately, we already know where this is headed. This belief is critical race theory on steroids. Where critical race theory and the Black Lives Matter Movement hold that racial problems are systemic, The 1619 Project goes further. The problem is not a few misguided, racist laws here and there. It is that slavery and its remnants are alive today. This is similar to the belief that police are hunting black men, once you accept this belief as a fact, no facts to the contrary will convince you otherwise.

In analyzing The 1619 Project, I will take two approaches. First, I will prove that the assertions made by the Project are false. There is plenty of evidence of this, and at times, I will use their own words to prove it. This is not always as easy as it seems, as they use several misleading tactics to convince their readers of the ominous racism that lurks in every corner. They sometimes cite indisputable facts, but draw out inferences to illogical conclusions; they take the lie-by-omission approach, leaving out relevant information; and they use bait-and-switch tactics. This is no way to make an argument if you have the facts on your side.

While I believe logic and context will win out, I do not think the strongest case is simply pointing out inaccuracies. This is where my second approach is key. In these cases, I give them their argument. I assume all their assumptions are true and say, "Now what?" Even if they are correct, what is the endgame of this racially biased teaching? I then take their argument to its logical end. I will apply these two approaches on each essay. I will start with the introduction.

Everyone knows, or they used to prior to the decline of our education system, about Plymouth Rock. In the Schoolhouse Rock video, *No More Kings*, the Mayflower is shown hitting a rock with the date 1620.[83] There are accounts of the Pilgrims and the unlikely assistance they received from Squanto, a Native American man from the Patuxet tribe. Even Hollywood director Spike Lee referenced it. In a famous line from his movie *X*,

83 "No More Kings," Schoolhouse Rock!, video archived online: https://www.youtube.com/watch?v=WvOZs3g3qIo

Malcolm X says, "We didn't land on Plymouth Rock, Plymouth Rock landed on us!"[84]

To convince America to view Jamestown, not the Plymouth landing, as the country's founding, there would need to be overwhelming evidence contradicting what has been accepted. The essayists provide no evidence; they simply deem it so, and, unfortunately, many will take their word. The question remains: If Plymouth is considered our founding and it was just one year after Jamestown, why make such a big deal about one year? America's vile, subhuman practice of chattel slavery does not disappear. Neither does the systemic racism of Jim Crow laws or the domestic terrorism of the Ku Klux Klan. The reason may seem subtle, but it is critical to their argument.

The reason The 1619 Project focuses on the Virginia colony is to place slaves within the colony in which the country traces its origin, thereby bolstering their argument that slavery was integral to the founding of America. Though Plymouth was only one year later, there were no slaves at its founding. In fact, the first recorded sale of a slave at Plymouth was 1685, sixty-five years later.[85] Focusing on Plymouth would debunk their "slave origins" narrative, so they simply "reframe" it.

To determine which colony is the true origin of America, we must first establish that the two colonies were different. At first glance, they may seem to be the same. Two colonies, founded by white Europeans, one year apart. How do we know they were

[84] Video clip from *X*, archived online at: https://www.youtube.com/watch?v=hMdDwBliS-o

[85] Patricia Scott Deetz, Christopher Fennell, and Jillian Galle, "The Plymouth Colony archive project," University of Illinois at Urbana-Champaign; website last modified December 14, 2007. http://www.histarch.illinois.edu/plymouth/Galle1.html

different? Here is how we know: The 1619 Project's founder and essayists tell us so. If the colonies were the same, there would be no effort on their part to push Jamestown as *the* founding colony. They would simply have made the same statements about Plymouth that they made about Jamestown. But they cannot say that because that lie would be too blatant.

Since we know the colonies were different, the only thing we need to do is confirm which is most clearly connected to America's founding. This can be determined by highlighting their differences and determining which is closer to American principles. Jamestown, and many other colonies, were founded either as extensions of a European monarchy or by someone granted the authority over the colonies. The Plymouth settlers came from Holland, not Britain, and were religious dissenters who had fled England. They were not connected to the crown. Their separation from the monarchy is huge in its significance, but it is not the only difference. There was also a difference in the colonies' governance.

There is a direct line from the nation's founding principles to the Plymouth colony. As Larry Schweikart, historian and author of *A Patriot's History of the United States*, explains, "American exceptionalism involves four 'pillars': 1) A Christian, mostly Protestant, religious foundation that has 'congregationalism' as its organizing force; 2) Common law, in which people believe God puts the law in the hearts of the people, and they elect leaders to enact those laws (vs. top down like 'Divine Right of Kings'), 3) Private property with written titles and deeds, and 4) a free market." Plymouth had all four; Jamestown did not.[86]

[86] Larry Schweikart and David Dougherty, *A Patriot's History of the Modern World*, 1st ed. (New York: Sentinel, 2012), 4.

It is obvious that the country the Founders wanted to create was more Plymouth than Jamestown. One year does not make much difference, but different ideas around structure and where laws come from are about as different as you can get. Any honest analysis will show that Plymouth is where America established its origin, and slaves were not a part of that beginning. The Project appropriately points out that the arrival of the slaves inaugurated a barbaric system of chattel slavery that would last for the next 250 years. However, it spread to the Plymouth colony much later, rather than getting its origin there, an important distinction which explains why they tried to negate it.

Here is an important aside. We cannot look at the colonies through the eyes of twenty-first-century Americans. Most Americans make the mistake of starting the calendar in 1776. We think of everyone in North America at the time as Americans. We forget that for more than half of the time between the original colonies and the Declaration of Independence, people were loyal to their homeland, and that homeland was not just Britain.

There was a fierce battle between France and Britain for control of the New World. Spain had its area of control, and to a smaller extent, so did the Dutch. In fact, they controlled New Amsterdam, an area they lost in battle with England, which was renamed New York, after the Duke of York. My point is that when slavery is discussed, no other country is given scrutiny. People rarely mention Britain, I assume because they see eventual Americans as British, but what about Spain, France, and the Netherlands? Not one mention, even though the Americans are the only ones in this group without slave ships.

Having established clear evidence of the country's colonial predecessor, I will now provide an example of my other approach. Let us assume they are right: that Jamestown was the model for America's founding, and slavery was present from the start. Would that prove that slaves were necessary to launch America? Because Jamestown, and America for that matter, *had* slavery does not mean that without slavery there could be no America.

If the principles adopted at Plymouth were the basis for its founding, America could still exist. The argument could be made that the country would not have grown as fast, but there is no evidence that it would not, and there is no reason to believe it would have failed completely. Keep in mind that Plymouth survived for decades without slavery. Additionally, some believe that slavery cost the country more wealth than it created, only making a small number of slaveowners rich and decimating the south. Either way, there is no evidence that slavery was necessary to start this country on its unique principles.

Anyone who makes this claim is revealing both a lack of understanding of human nature and dismissal of foundational biblical principles. Man is flawed, and there is no limit to the evil some will do. Those at The 1619 Project believe that one *must* be anti-black to subjugate and dehumanize people the way blacks were done under chattel slavery. To disprove this, one only needs to look at the Nazis.

The Nazis were evil and had a toxic, unnatural hatred for the Jews. But they were but a small group of people. To infect others with their hatred, they used propaganda to spread lies and create the environment where people became hostile against Jews. Once the foundation was laid, they sold the German people on the fact that Jews were *Untermensch*, or subhuman. This led to millions of dead Jews, including hundreds of thousands tortured and experimented on. Was this because of anti-black racism?

What about the genocide in Rwanda or the Holodomor in Ukraine? Here again, millions killed in Ukraine, none of them black, while in Rwanda, both the victims and the murderers were black. Are we to believe the Hutus had a mutated strain of anti-black racism? These are global horrors, but one need not use a global example. Think of serial killers or kidnappers. Many of them kill and hold captive people who look like them. Racism is real, but it is not a prerequisite for immoral and brutal behavior. This includes slavery.

Even if I concede that slavery was a necessary ingredient in the recipe of America, there would still be a serious problem with the conclusion The 1619 Project draws from it. The editor-in-chief takes a grandiose leap by stating, in no uncertain terms, that *everything* exceptional about America grew out of slavery. The examples he uses sets up the arguments made by the essayists throughout the project. I will address each individually as I analyze the essays, but I would like to make two observations about this conclusion.

The first is that Silverstein made an amazing concession, albeit unwittingly. In his effort to highlight the significance of black influence on America, he admitted that American exceptionalism exists. He said, "everything truly exceptional" came out of slavery. This is an interesting choice of words coming from a member of a group that only highlights the bad in America. This leads to my second point. Emphasizing the horrors of slavery is fair, but they go so far as to imply that whites contributed nothing. Based on their interpretations, everything developed in America was either made by slaves and stolen by whites or created by luck. Slavery is the only contribution made by whites.

This is the first step in getting fair-minded Americans to accept "progressive racism." Sympathy toward blacks is not enough. You need to paint an extreme narrative; you need anger; you need horror. If white police officers are indiscriminately shooting blacks, that is horrific. If slavery, its de facto replacement, Jim Crow, and systemic racism is holding the majority of blacks back today, we need to be angry. Once you convince people that the extremes you describe are true, it is not a stretch to get them to agree that extreme measures should be taken to fix them. The problem is that the facts do not fit their narrative.

As with Black Lives Matter's police brutality argument, this "all roads lead to slavery" approach collapses under the weight of fact and logic. The essays imply, and sometimes state directly, that every white American has benefitted from slavery. This includes every white American from 1619 through today, regardless of family origin, education, or income level. The arbitrary claim is completely implausible yet, like all arbitrary claims, impossible to disprove. There is no way to track the effects of every profit, job, or legal decision a white person has benefitted from and confirm, or disprove, its link to slavery.

While on average, whites fare better in most quality-of-life categories, there are many who are unemployed, homeless, addicted to drugs, in prison, or living in poverty. What is the Project saying about them, since they are supposedly enjoying "white privilege" despite their situations? Many in the progressive racism crowd would say that white privilege cannot protect you from the consequences of your bad decisions. That is fair, and the same should be said to blacks about their bad behavior. But only the latter are given the shield of slavery to hide behind.

What The 1619 Project makes clear for blacks is: Even if you work hard and achieve success in America, you worked harder than whites and would likely be more successful if you hadn't been held back by the lingering effects of slavery. Worse, if you do not achieve the success you wanted, it is likely because of the racist system.

I do not like to use the "victim" label, but this argument is getting awfully close to it. I honestly do not think it's intentional. I believe the goal is to guilt whites into giving blacks something: reparations, set-asides, career preferences, something. This built-in excuse for failing is just an unintended consequence. Now, the racial lines are drawn. The system is stacked against blacks, and whites just breeze through life enjoying opportunities blacks could only dream of having.

How do you bring about the equality everyone truly deserves? You cannot stop racism, as many idealists suggest. They are trying to eliminate a belief or feeling. You cannot legislate it away or "erase" it. They also make the mistake of assuming racism exists in every situation that ends without their desired outcome. They are being led by their emotions, which can easily get out of control. This is how otherwise intelligent people can be driven to illogical conclusions and extreme reactions.

It sounds far-fetched, but the only way to give them what they want is to repeal and replace the Civil Rights Act of 1964. They will frame it as the only way to achieve equality. They are preparing the country for racial set-asides. These social justice warriors would have no problem with quotas, or specific laws for blacks. They have already started the shift. We have "progressed" to separate graduations, separate dorm rooms, and BIPOC (the latest in the left's newspeak—it means Black, Indigenous, and People of Color) spaces. They are saying, in no uncertain terms, that segregation is fine as long as it is initiated by blacks.

Regardless of your opinion of these race-focused movements, they are extremely effective. Some will support them because they are naïve enough to believe they are helping. You can also always count on appeasers to latch on to these types of movements. Corporations, for example, have no conscience and will donate to anything that will help the bottom line. There will always be members of the group slated to benefit who will acquiesce or remain silent, thinking it will not harm them. They are wrong.

The 1619 Project and movements like it cannot work no matter how much support they garner. First, like their counterparts at Black Lives Matter, they are too focused on the response of whites. They are essentially saying that the country needs to change, and all that change needs to come from whites. If your success is predicated on someone else reacting, you have no control over your movement and its destiny. If the effects of slavery are truly pervasive today, they have caused damage to the black community. If the black community is damaged, then it needs repair. However, that repair cannot come from whites alone. Yet, there is no directive by the Project to "reframe" the black community.

If racism is the main reason blacks are poor, giving them money is not going to teach them financial management. If racism makes blacks angry, causing them to commit crimes, criminal justice reform is not going to teach them anger management. Assuming racism caused obesity by creating "food deserts," mandating healthy options in black communities will not change eating habits. If racism is the reason black children are lagging behind all others in academic achievement, adding The 1619 Project to their curriculum won't teach them what they need to succeed in the world. It will only cause them to view themselves as perpetual victims, which will further exacerbate the problem.

In this section, I will examine The 1619 Project as I did the Black Lives Matter movement, exposing factual inaccuracies and using their words to give context and a clear understanding of what they are saying and what it means. Each Project essay has a different writer and discusses a different topic, but they coalesce on the same premise. To keep readers focused on the 400-year lie, each essay is embedded with a link to this statement:

> The 1619 Project is an ongoing initiative from The New York Times Magazine that began in August 2019, the 400th anniversary of the beginning of American slavery. It aims to reframe the country's history by placing the consequences of slavery and the contributions of black Americans at the very center of our national narrative. Read all the stories.

Honest readers will see that the Project is based on a false premise and highlights few contributions of black Americans. It is anti-American propaganda cloaked in pro-black pseudo-history. The most disturbing part is that by accepting the Project's premises and admitting its materials into our schools, we are helping them destroy the country. Like the Trojans, we open the gates to the horse, only to find racists waiting inside.

This section will conclude with a call to action. I bill myself as a solutions guy. I believe if you are talking about a problem and not offering solutions, you are just wasting time. I will give readers steps they can take to immediately push back against these black-focused movements.

The first step is knowing what you are up against. The 1619 Project is reframing American history to make it solely synonymous with slavery. They are succeeding at making this perspective mainstream and bringing this toxic approach to the classroom. We owe it to our children and our country to stop them.

12

The Idea of America

Our democracy's founding ideals were false when they were written. Black Americans have fought to make them true.
—Nikole Hannah-Jones

The first and most important essay of The 1619 Project was written by Nikole Hannah-Jones, a staff writer for the *New York Times*, and the founder of the Project. Where my previous chapter summarized the Project, as presented by the magazine's editor, this chapter will serve as a detailed explanation of the genesis of the Project and its alleged importance to the fabric of America.

Hannah-Jones's essay, "America Wasn't a Democracy Until Black Americans Made It One," is about slavery's origins in America and its effects on black Americans today. It is well-written, detailed in some areas, vague in others. There are plenty of facts in her essay, and while the ugliness of slavery and racism are vividly detailed, she could have been even more graphic and presented a greater volume of examples if inclined. This cannot be disputed. What she is missing, though, and what the entire 1619 Project is lacking, is logic and context.

The shortsightedness of the Project has less to do with the quality of the research or the intellect of the presenters than it does with the emotionally clouded judgment applied to the information gathered. They were not seeking truth; they were seeking confirmation bias. A common tactic used in most of the essays is to start with a fact, but weave their opinions into it. This would not be a problem if they did not present their opinions as fact. One example is the case of Hiram Rhodes Revels.

Hiram Rhodes Revels was the first black American elected to the U.S. Senate. Prior to his mention, the essay states, "…they [black voters] headed in droves to the polls, where they placed other formerly enslaved people into seats that their enslavers had once held." This implies that black voters catapulted Revels to the Senate. What the essay fails to mention is that U.S. Senators were elected by state legislatures, and since Senator Revels was elected in February of 1870—weeks after Mississippi ratified the Fifteenth Amendment and a month before the Constitution was amended—his election was won with the votes of only whites.

This distortion of history is an example of why this Project is so dangerous. The essays are gripping; they tell compelling stories of the putrid hatred and violence many innocent blacks experienced at the hands of whites. They chronicle actions government officials took that hurt blacks, many of them intentional, and the long shadows they cast, as well as the overt racism of white citizens these legislators condoned or permitted. But the Project is woefully incomplete. It does not present any positives, only occasional examples of blacks overcoming obstacles. In their telling, few whites did anything right, and even they benefitted from slavery, so they were also bad.

This is intellectually lazy. It cheats the reader and anyone it is presented to as an educational tool. Many may not be aware that The 1619 Project is being implemented as history or social studies curriculum in many public-school districts and some private schools with "woke" administrators. The argument is that American history courses currently being taught are limited and highly glossed. In some ways, this is true. Unfortunately, the education they are proposing is just as limiting; it is also solely negative about America, overly race-focused, and more opinion than fact. As Hannah-Jones pointed out on Twitter:

> I've said consistently that The 1619 Project is AN origin story, not THE origin story. Our intro says explicitly, what *would* it mean to consider 1619 our founding—not that it IS our founding.[87]

Whatever your views on this project, fair-minded people should agree that introducing this as "history" and teaching it in schools is highly inappropriate. It is loosely based on highly selective facts and presents a one-sided interpretation of America. But America is made up of many unique stories, and most differ from this negative narrative. We are at a time in our country where we are regressing to the racial divide they claim to oppose. The Black Lives Matter movement, white-guilt advocates, and

---

87 Nikole Hannah-Jones Twitter post reshared here: https://twitter.com/redsteeze/status/1287987731721646082/photo/1

The 1619 Project are a powerful triumvirate propagated toxic myths into America's cultural mainstream.

This is what Nikole Hannah-Jones describes in her essay.

Hannah-Jones opens her essay with a confusing view of America from her childhood: her father's patriotism. She describes how he proudly flew the flag, always pristine, despite the home's exterior needing repair. She goes on to describe her family history, common among black Americans: a family of sharecroppers living in segregated Mississippi. Because of the lack of freedom and the threat of lynching, her grandmother moved the family to Iowa in the 1940s. There she faced the same segregation and job discrimination she hoped to avoid in the South.

Her father joined the Army, she states, to escape poverty, but also in the hopes that his service would afford him better treatment by whites. His condition did not change in the Army, and he would labor in service jobs for the rest of his life. Hannah-Jones says she could not understand how her father saw firsthand how blacks were abused, but still flew the flag. She was "deeply embarrassed" by his patriotism. She caps this off by confessing she was taught in school "that the flag wasn't really ours, that our history as a people began with enslavement and that we had contributed little to this great nation." This gives us a glimpse into the origins of her skewed view of America.

I want to contrast this with my father's story—a similar story with a completely different ending. My father was born and spent his formative years in Oklahoma, a land where another group of people was subjugated: Native Americans. The area, known as Indian Territory, is where many native people were driven like cattle by the U.S. government. What most Americans do not know is that many of those Native Americans owned black slaves[88] and thousands were brought with them on the "Trail of Tears."[89] My dad, like many black Okies, was a descendant of one of those slaves.

Like Hannah-Jones, my paternal grandparents moved north, setting in East Chicago, Illinois, and my father also joined the Army. Here is where things change. My father went to an integrated high school where many of his friends were white. He undoubtedly experienced racism but made it clear to my brothers and me that people are complicated. He told me, "There are good and bad people in every class and race; assume the good but be prepared for the bad." Basically, he was instilling in me the Russian proverb "trust, but verify" before Reagan made it famous.[90] It is interesting to note that my father was born in 1920. When Hannah-Jones's father was born in 1945, my father was being honorably discharged from the Army.

People are shaped by their experiences. Hannah-Jones and I were both raised in segregated neighborhoods, but I did not live a segregated life. I saw my father interact with whites as friends and

---

88 Ryan P. Smith, "How Native American slaveholders complicate the Trail of Tears narrative," *Smithsonian Magazine,* March 6, 2018. https://www.smithsonianmag.com/smithsonian-institution/how-native-american-slaveholders-complicate-trail-tears-narrative-180968339/

89 Tiya Miles, "Pain of 'Trail of Tears' shared by Blacks as well as Native Americans," CNN, February 25, 2012. https://www.cnn.com/2012/02/25/us/pain-of-trail-of-tears-shared-by-blacks-as-well-as-native-americans/index.html

90 Nikolay Shevchenko, "Did Reagan really coin the term, 'Trust but verify,' a proverb revived by HBO's Chernobyl?," *Russia Beyond,* June 17, 2019. https://www.rbth.com/lifestyle/330521-reagan-trust-but-verify-chernobyl

equals, not in a subservient role. As a young child, my grandparents moved back to the South, settling in a small town in North Texas. There were few blacks there, so when we traveled there in the summers, nearly all the children I played with were white. I remember playing with a group of children one day. The next day, one of them said we could not play together because I was black. I shrugged my shoulders and kept playing with the rest of the kids. I must have channeled my dad.

The biggest difference between our two stories is the education experience. She was bused to a majority-white school. The teacher she described was obviously white. I went to black schools with mostly black teachers. They did not unethically infuse their opinions into our education, and they would never have made a racist, self-defeating, and factually inaccurate statement in the classroom. My teachers were children of the civil rights movement, and they were able to convey a love of America and black people. Obviously, Hannah-Jones missed this.

There is one other thing I believe she was missing. There is a view among blacks that is widely believed but rarely written about or talked about in "mixed company." I must preface this by saying that I don't present this as history or a psychological analysis, but the observation is common enough that it can bring insight to the nuances within black America and give color to the way Hannah-Jones sees black history.

When I read her essay, I paid close attention to the portions about her family background, as they likely shaped her views. After reading her examples from school and thinking about what she wrote earlier about her dad and grandmama, I immediately searched her background and confirmed what I was thinking.

Her mother is white.

White readers are probably wondering where I got that from, while blacks are silently saying, "I thought the same thing!" Biracial kids have a somewhat unique experience, as you can probably imagine. Most of them identify as black, but some have a bit of an identity crisis.

Most biracial kids who struggle with their identity find a way to deal with it when they get older, but those who struggle often have difficulties embracing their blackness. They are left with a longing to connect with the black community in the same way most blacks do. They feel a distant closeness to their blackness. They have a sort of one-sided romantic relationship with it. This is intensified in children who do not grow up in majority-black neighborhoods, or those who grow up in families with financial comfort. For them, blackness, and the injustices against it, are magnified.

For most blacks, being black is who we are; for them, it is a character they play. They must be convincing in their roles, even if it means they must discount or show hatred toward one of their parents. Barack Obama grew up with his white grandparents but wrote about his father. Colin Kaepernick grew up in a white middle-class family, yet he is solely focused on the black community. Hannah-Jones seems to have the same affliction.

This problem was apparently exacerbated by her schooling. Because she was taught that blacks contributed nothing, she went in search of contributions and over-corrected. This is why several black activists, from Malcolm X to Claud Anderson, did not think integration was the answer.[91] As Bob Woodson, founder

[91] Dr. Claud Anderson and Dr. Boyd Watkins, "Financial Juneteenth: The Resurrection of Black America," April 20, 2017, film excerpt posted at: https://www.youtube.com/watch?v=uv2KfLPQcdM

of 1776 Unites, says, "The opposite of segregation is desegregation, not integration." They fought for equality and believed people should have the freedom to choose where and how they live. They did not think it meant transporting blacks into "white life." In the aggregate, it was a net good, but integration did have some unintended consequences; beliefs like those espoused by Hannah-Jones are among them.

Her teachers were terrible stewards of their students. Their teachings went against both the founding ideals of America and the ethical responsibilities of their job. They should not have passed their negative beliefs onto their students. Unfortunately, this has gone full circle as Hannah-Jones's Project is repeating that cycle. The entire Project focuses only on America's flaws. This will bring nothing but misery to all involved. Why should people who hold contempt for the country be allowed to educate our children, particularly about the country they despise?

Hannah-Jones's family and teachers failed her by letting her believe that she, and children like her, had limited opportunities in the country. Think about the country she describes, then juxtapose that with her actual life. A black woman who is the daughter of a black man who worked "service jobs" for most of his life. Yet not only is she successful, but her success grew exponentially when she started pointing out how the effects of slavery are pervasive in America today. How ironic. Not only is she allowed to call the country racist, but the "oppressor" elevates her onto a high-visibility platform to do so, helping to push her anti-white narrative.

After using her family history to show the difficulties of the black experience in America, Hannah-Jones shifts to her American origin narrative. She starts with the Jamestown colony, and the 1619 entry of slaves that I debunked as our founding in the previous chapter.

But there is a lot missing from her historical recounting, making it difficult for the average American, much less public school students, to grasp an adequate understanding of the complex information provided, or discern whether or not the conclusions she draws are logical. I will add the necessary context. I often point out how writers with an agenda omit information necessary to analyze the clarity of their argument. This is a tactic frequently used by Hannah-Jones. Unfortunately, in many cases, you must already know the facts to catch it. Other times, you only need to pay attention.

When describing the grueling journey of the Middle Passage, the transporting of kidnapped and purchased African slaves to the New World, she mentioned that as many as 12.5 million Africans would be migrated. She then, correctly, states that 400,000 slaves were sold into America. What happened to the other 12.1 million?

One would think the fact that over 96 percent of all Africans forced into the transatlantic slave trade struggled somewhere other than America would be essential information to an "origin" story. I will concede that the 400,000 number grew exponentially due to the horrific practice of forcing slaves to procreate in order to create a lineage of slavery; but to spend so much time focused on slavery and its lingering effects, and only address the plight of four percent, exemplifies the lack of honest historical accounts throughout the Project. This confirms my argument that the absence of contempt for Great Britain, Spain, France, Portugal, and the Netherlands is not an oversight; it is by design.

Next, she levels an attack on capitalism. She gives many accounts of the ways in which slave labor was used to help the country advance. Prominent figures, industry leaders, the government, and prestigious universities all benefitted from the stolen labor of slaves. This is undeniable, but it may be the only time Hannah-Jones underestimated its depths.

She ties these profits to the Founders and other whites, but in fact, almost everyone living at that time was complicit in these evil practices. The Africans who sold the slaves, the slave traders, the Europeans, Asians, and Caribbean traders who bought the raw materials or sold the wares. It is not American capitalism, as they call it, that is the problem; it is the realities of the world from the sixteenth through nineteenth century that are to blame.

She then goes on to defend against an attack no one levies, saying that it would be historically inaccurate to reduce the contributions of black people to the wealth created in bondage. This is a depiction of blacks only her teachers would claim.

Then, she focuses on her main target: the Founders. Her claim is that the United States was founded on "both an ideal and a lie." This is a common belief of those who cannot see past their emotions to apply context to the realities of the world in the eighteenth century. They view America through a narrow lens, unaware, or intentionally ignoring, the fact that slavery was ubiquitous. Remember the 96 percent of Africans scattered elsewhere? Well, there were also Africans enslaved by other Africans, as well as non-African slaves throughout Europe and Asia.

Understanding that slavery was the rule and not the exception of the time is important. But there was another universal truth in the eighteenth century: the lack of democratically elected rulers. Every country had either a monarch, despot, oligarch, or tribal leader. There was no system of government where the people elected leaders to represent them.

However, everything changed with the founding of America. The idea of America—the rights of individuals—and its central role in our founding documents have influenced the constitutions of nearly every country in the world.[92] This is the reason the Founders are celebrated here and throughout the world, not for their sins.

This is the fatal flaw of those who try to soil the idea of America by exposing hypocrisy in its Founders. Hannah-Jones and her essayists would have you believe that the personal sins of the Founders make the country irredeemable. They owned slaves, and that is all we need to know. She dedicates more time in her essay detailing the Founders' profits and slave counts than she does discussing their actual views on slavery. The most prominent Founders wrote often about their views on slavery, yet not one of these quotes made their way into The 1619 Project. Here are just a few.

> George Washington—*There is not a man living who wishes more sincerely than I do, to see a plan adopted for the abolition of it.*

> Benjamin Franklin—*Slavery is such an atrocious debasement of human nature, that its very extirpation, if not performed with solicitous care, may sometimes open a source of serious evils.*

---

92 Albert P. Blaustein, "Influence of the American Constitution abroad," Encyclopedia.com; entry published in 1986. https://www.encyclopedia.com/politics/encyclopedias-almanacs-transcripts-and-maps/influence-american-constitution-abroad

> Thomas Jefferson—*Be assured that no person living wishes more sincerely than I do, to see a complete refutation of the doubts I have myself entertained and expressed on the grade of understanding allotted to them by nature, and to find that in this respect they are on a par with ourselves. My doubts were the result of personal observation on the limited sphere of my own State, where the opportunities for the development of their genius were not favorable...but whatever be their degree of talent it is no measure of their rights.*

These quotes clearly described an awareness of the immoral debasement of slavery. Significantly, these are words from the Founders who owned slaves. Though Hannah-Jones does not mention it, several of the Founders were abolitionists and never owned slaves. Her argument, and that of many people who present the Founders as one-dimensional, is that they did not believe what they wrote. They point to not only the fact that they did not add the abolition of slavery to the Constitution, but they continued the practice personally.

However, as difficult as it is to admit, adding such language *at that time* would have impeded the country's creation.

Hannah-Jones argues that slavery was omitted from the Constitution because the Framers understood their hypocrisy. The truth is more complicated. While slaves were still held in all thirteen colonies in 1776, many states were quickly moving toward abolitions. However, the five Southern states were steadfast in protecting the practice and would not have joined the Union if slavery were abolished. Without their cooperation, there would be no Declaration of Independence.

Some historians believe that slavery would have ended sooner had the British won the Revolutionary War. It is impossible to know, but the theory is possible since Great Britain abolished slavery decades before the United States, yet they still had a monarchy. There is no way to know when or if the ideals that underpin our system of government would have been implemented. Besides, with the South being so pro-slavery, they may well have fought to keep it and enforced Jim Crow laws anyway. And for those who think discrimination would have ended, as of this writing, the Black Lives Matter movement is in London making the same demands they are making in America.

Pointing out these facts inevitably earns you the label of "white apologist" from proponents of black-focused movements. I make it clear that my goal is sharing the truth in a logical way. My efforts to explain the facts about the country's founding should not be taken as whitewashing the Founders' beliefs. While I think their writings are important, there is no doubt that they believed in the superiority of whites. The reality—it is possible to believe blacks are inferior yet not believe they should be property.

An objective view of the Founders will show that they were men who would have been considered elites in their time. In their writings, they referenced Aristotle, Cicero, John Locke, and the Bible. Like the other elites of their times, and in times since, they believed they had a higher calling. "All have natural rights, but some are more equipped to lead" would describe their view. While they were creating a more perfect union, they were not perfect. Most Americans know about women's suffrage, but few know that white men who did not own property did not earn the right to vote until 1828. It was an exclusive club.

As I stated in my *RealClearPolitics* essay on the Declaration of Independence, "Besides, the best argument against slavery is the Declaration of Independence itself. If all men are created equal, then blacks cannot be excluded. If our rights are endowed by the Creator, they cannot be given or taken away by arbitrary leaders."[93]

After nearly one hundred years, slavery ended in the United States. The racists clung so ardently to the institution that we had to fight a war to end it. Hannah-Jones will have you believe that Lincoln's opposition was to secession, not the enslavement of blacks. This is partly true, but as is common throughout The 1619 Project, it is a cherry-picked fact to fit their narrative. Lincoln did say, "If I could save the union without freeing a slave I would," but that was in the context of illustrating how badly he wanted the union maintained.

Though his views evolved, he did not see blacks as equals, but that does not mean he did not think slavery should be abolished. Here is a portion of his response to the Supreme Court's decision on the Dred Scott case. He made the remarks four years before the start of the Civil War, in response to Justice Douglas, who accused Republicans of wanting to marry Negroes:

> Now I protest against that counterfeit logic, which concludes that, because I do not want a black woman for a slave, I must necessarily want her for a wife. I need not have her for either, I can just leave her alone. In some respects, she certainly is not my equal, but in her natural right to eat the bread she earns with her own hands

---

93 Charles Love, "An Independence Day message for Black Americans," *RealClearPolitics*, July 3, 2020. https://www.realclearpolitics.com/articles/2020/07/03/an_independence_day_message_for_black_americans_143612.html

> without asking leave of anyone else, she is my equal, and the equal of all others.

Regardless, over 600,000 men died to end slavery, yet The 1619 Project would have you believe that all of them held contempt for black people.

The end of the war ushered in Reconstruction. Here is the only area in which Hannah-Jones had anything positive to say, and even that was skewed. Her take on Reconstruction? Blacks fighting for human rights and organizing people to vote. She celebrated the fact that within ten years of the end of the Civil War, sixteen black men served in Congress, and more than six hundred black men served in Southern state legislatures. The years directly after slavery saw the greatest expansion of human and civil rights this nation would ever see, and according to Jones it was, "Led by black activists and a Republican Party pushed left...."

This description is a not-so-veiled attempt to separate those Republicans from today's Republicans and to suggest that they were liberal ("left"). What she fails to mention is that the Republicans she gives credit to were called the Radical Republicans; they were opposed by the Liberal Republicans. Either way, she says that the positive advances did not last because anti-black racism runs "in the very DNA of this country." There are obvious flaws in this argument and too many important facts that are being overlooked in Hannah-Jones's account of the Reconstruction Period in America.

The first is that she only highlights the work of blacks. While their achievements were amazing, especially considering where they were just a few years prior, they represented a small percentage of the accomplishments during that period. She attributes political victories to blacks, but like Senator Revels's election, most of the legal advances she celebrated were passed with few or no black votes. The Civil Rights Act of 1866, for example, was passed in Congress after overriding President Andrew Johnson's veto, four years before blacks won the right to vote in the Constitution.

The most notable omission from Hannah-Jones' section on Reconstruction was that of Ulysses S. Grant. He was a two-term president whose entire presidency was during the Reconstruction Era. He decimated the Klan, signed several civil rights acts into law, and ushered in the Fifteenth Amendment to the Constitution, granting former slaves full citizenship. It is shocking that she would give a review of the Reconstruction Era without one mention of Grant, but was able to squeeze in President Hayes's various failures.

Similarly, she points out the battle for equal rights and the racist whites who opposed them, as well as the abhorrent violence and immoral debasement of the subsequent Jim Crow laws, but she assumes this racism to reflect the beliefs of all whites. Her "DNA" comment makes her views of whites clear. But how does this analysis comport with President Grant's actions or those of his cabinet? Or those of the politicians who overwhelmingly voted in favor of civil rights for blacks? Keep in mind they had enough votes to override a presidential veto. That is a lot of racist DNA supporting the rights of blacks.

Because they settled on a singular view of America they want to promulgate, The 1619 Project skews heavily on the subjugation of blacks and minimizes the actions of those whites who fought for true human rights or took actions to increase opportunities for blacks. Instead, this is how Hannah-Jones prefers to show America:

> In response to black demands for these rights, white Americans strung them from trees, beat them and dumped their bodies in muddy rivers, assassinated them in their front yards, firebombed them on buses, mauled them with dogs, peeled back their skin with fire hoses and murdered their children with explosives set off inside a church.

In *her* "memory," it wasn't *some* whites who did these things, it was "white Americans." And the attacks were on *all* blacks. She's right about the evils of slavery, the domestic terrorism of the Ku Klux Klan, and the regressive, racist policies of Jim Crow; but she ignores any positives about whites in an effort to make the negatives universal. Unfortunately, as strong as blacks are, our great achievements in America would not have been possible, or would have been greatly delayed, without the support from whites she aims to erase from history.

Congress established the Freedmen's Bureau to help former slaves and poor whites after the Civil War, as well as approving land grants for historically black colleges and universities (HBCU). Wealthy whites like Rockefeller and Rosenwald, believing education was the key to success, funded many schools for blacks. Many also sacrificed their lives. Painting whites with a broad "racist" brush sullies the legacy and efforts of people like Amos Dresser and the Lane Rebels, Elijah Lovejoy, John W. Stephens, Andrew Goodman, Michael Schwerner, and many more.

There are many other examples of whites taking steps to improve the lives of blacks, as well as pushing back against the virulent racism that existed, albeit limited, throughout America, but the best argument against her depiction of all whites as racist is Hannah-Jones's own words. She listed what she called egalitarian state constitutions and the expansion of human and civil rights. Who does she think passed these constitutions and laws?

While these expansions did not last, logic would suggest that if anti-black racism were in the DNA of America, these expansions would not have been accomplished at all. Though her writing suggests universal white hatred for blacks, she may argue that she does not mean all whites. That may be the case, but there is no doubt she means the majority. Yet if this were the case, how did the Republicans, a party founded on the abolition of slavery, win control of all three branches of government in 1864?

Even the implementation of Jim Crow laws, racist as they were, does not prove racism among all citizens. We look back at businesses following these practices and assumed the owners and managers agreed with them, but this was not always the case. Take, for example, the segregation of streetcars in the South. In "The Political Economy of Segregation: The Case of Segregated Streetcars," Jennifer Roback studied the implementation of these laws and found that many companies did not agree with the practice and some actively resisted them. Roback wrote:

> My evidence suggests that segregation laws did not simply codify an already existing, well-established social custom. On the contrary, contemporary reports indicate that whites and blacks customarily sat where they chose on municipal streetcars in the absence of segregation ordinances. Second, the streetcar companies frequently resisted segregation, both as custom and law. In addition, there is little indication that

> pressure for segregation came from the average white passenger.[94]

I will discuss more about the economics of this in my chapter on the Project's capitalism essay. What the evidence shows is the ugly truth of the human condition. A small number of people pushed a radical idea, and it gained some support; though they did not represent most people, too many who opposed it said nothing. Politicians moved to support the squeaky wheels. This served as negative racial training, making things worse. Younger whites grew up learning to focus on racial differences.

But this is exactly what the Black Lives Matter movement and The 1619 Project are doing.

To prove my point, Hannah-Jones makes the argument that slavery and the continued inhumanity visited upon blacks by Jim Crow and other racist laws were necessary for whites to justify the country's past. In her twisted logic, if former slaves and their dependents thrived and became equals in society, "then the entire justification for how this nation allowed slavery would collapse. Free black people posed a danger to the country's idea of itself as exceptional."

She continues by arguing that blacks fought alone. If her essay were based on historical facts, when she rightfully describes the brutality and, in certain areas, commonality of lynching, she would acknowledge that though it was a practice that was overwhelmingly inflicted on blacks without provocation, many whites died alongside them. Of the 4,000 who were lynched,

---

[94] Jennifer Roback, "The political economy of segregation: The case of segregated streetcars," *The Journal of Economic History,* Vol. XLVI, No. 4, December 1986, pp. 893–917. https://www.jstor.org/stable/2121814

more than one-third were white, most killed for supporting black rights. But since she is "reimagining," she can ignore this as well.

Another group she forgets is the suffragettes. Many white women, whose rights were also limited, fought on behalf of blacks. Susan B. Anthony, Elizabeth Cady Stanton, and others understood the importance of freedom for all.

Not surprisingly, those focused on race are not impressed. Recently, the country celebrated the centennial of the passage of women's suffrage. President Trump gave Susan B. Anthony a posthumous pardon.[95] She had been arrested for illegally voting and fined one hundred dollars, which she did not pay. The president was summarily attacked for his symbolic gesture. This came as no surprise. The surprising reactions were the attacks on Susan B. Anthony.

There were articles and social media posts arguing that Susan B. Anthony, and other suffragettes, were racist and fought against blacks. This is not entirely true. Anthony and Stanton formed the American Equal Rights Association with Frederick Douglass. They fought for the rights of women and blacks. Most omitted this from their attacks, but those who acknowledged it claimed that the suffragettes changed and began working with white supremacists. Others argued that some of their marches were segregated.

This may be true, but context is everything. This supposed shift happened after black men won the right to vote. Keep in mind—black men, five years after being treated as property,

[95] Geoff Herbert, "Who was Susan B. Anthony? President Trump officially pardons Upstate NY suffragist," Syracuse.com, August 19, 2020. https://www.syracuse.com/state/2020/08/who-was-susan-b-anthony-president-trump-officially-pardons-upstate-ny-suffragist.html

secured the right to vote in 1870. This was fifty years before women would be allowed to vote. It seems like they were bitter about this. Two groups fight together for equal rights, yet one is granted while the other is left wanting. It is more likely that their approach shifted because the landscape shifted.

Selfishness seems a better argument than racism. We are to believe that these women thought blacks should be afforded dignity, then suddenly decided they were wrong. The other complaint was that they worked with white supremacists. This does not make a person racist; they are simply aligning themselves with anyone they feel can help their cause. What is most interesting is that the suffragettes are being attacked for doing exactly what the progressive racists are doing: putting their goals ahead of everyone else's.

As if the fallacy of blacks fighting alone for their rights was not enough, Hannah-Jones all but demands a thank you from every other "identity" group. She claims that women and Native Americans got equality because of the struggle of blacks. I do not understand where Hannah-Jones derives this line of thinking. We have already established that women fought a long battle for equal rights, continuing for decades after black men won theirs. Native Americans resisted enslavement and fought for equality through forced removal, assimilation, and the denial of the vote. They did not get the right to vote in every state until 1962. To say that everyone's freedom stems from the fight of blacks is disingenuous and shows extreme hubris.

Next, she sets her sights on immigrants. She argues that the civil rights movement is the reason immigrants can come to America. There is no evidence for this. Immigrants basically came freely as companies needed to fill jobs. Plantations in Hawaii, the gold rush in California, and laying tracks on the railroads—the opportunities were endless until whites argued their wages were being driven down. In 1882, Chinese immigration was prohibited.[96] Other South Asian immigrants took their place until they, too, were blocked by the Asiatic Barred Zone Act of 1917.[97]

This practice of biased immigration laws continued for nearly thirty years, limiting access and suppressing the rights of those who were admitted. Things began to change independently of the struggle for rights by blacks. President Franklin D. Roosevelt accelerated this shift, forcing thousands of Japanese Americans into internment camps during World War II. Regardless of what caused the shift, Hannah-Jones's mindset on immigration is regressive and as racist as those who excluded Chinese immigrants.

Recently, Asian-American students have found themselves singled out for discriminatory treatment in both high school and college, based solely on their race. In New York City, there are eight elite public schools that accept students solely on their performance on an admission test. Mayor Bill de Blasio promised change when it was reported that Asian-American students represent 62 percent of the students at the elite schools. Conversely, black and Hispanic students represent only 9 percent of the student body but 70 percent of the city's population. The mayor

---

96 History.com staff, "Chinese Exclusion Act," History.com, August 24, 2018; updated September 13, 2019. https://www.history.com/topics/immigration/chinese-exclusion-act-1882

97 "Immigration Act of 1917." http://www.immigrationtounitedstates.org/588-immigration-act-of-1917.html

promised to "reserve" 20 percent of the seats at the school for diversity students. The Asian-American students are suing.[98]

Harvard University is undergoing a similar lawsuit. Harvard's goal, like that of the elite high schools in New York City, is to admit more black and Hispanic students. Asian-American students are suing the school, alleging that Asian-American applicants are being held to a higher standard than applicants from other races, creating a de facto quota system.[99] These students have put in the hard work over many years to get into these schools and feel it is unfair to pass on them simply because of their race. All they want is to be treated with equality, but this does not sit well with Hannah-Jones. She specifically addressed this in her essay, stating:

> It is a truly American irony that some Asian-Americans, among the groups able to immigrate to the United States because of the black civil rights struggle, are now suing universities to end programs designed to help the descendants of the enslaved.

The fact that many Asian-American immigrants were here decades before the Civil Rights Act of 1964 should disprove her

---

98 Lindsey Christ, "Asian-American parents file lawsuit against the city," Spectrum News NY1, December 13, 2018. https://www.ny1.com/nyc/all-boroughs/news/2018/12/14/asian-american-parents-file-lawsuit-against-the-city

99 Katie Reilly, "A lawsuit by Asian-American students against Harvard could end affirmative action as we know it," *TIME*, October 16, 2018. https://time.com/5425147/harvard-affirmative-action-trial-asian-american-students/

claim that they were able to immigrate because of the black civil rights struggle. This is an odd response for someone supposedly fighting for equality to make. But anyone who understands Hannah-Jones and her Project would not be surprised. We know this is just another example of their desire to justify their calls for black preference.

She goes on to imply that blacks have a greater claim to the ideals of the country. This only proves that she does not understand the Declaration of Independence or its ideals. Everyone's claim to this country is equal: from the immigrants sworn in as citizens at the 2020 Republican National Convention to the Daughters of the American Revolution, they all have the same claim to the flag. She then lists several liberal policies blacks are more likely to support, as if that strengthens their claims to America. She saves her most disingenuous claim for last, saying, "Black people have seen the worst of America, yet, somehow, we still believe in its best." If this were true, the Black Lives Matter movement and The 1619 Project would not exist, and she would have something positive to say about America.

Hannah-Jones continues her essay with a convoluted explanation of black culture. She begins by saying that the enslaved Africans had their cultures stolen away from them, so they had to create a culture of their own. This much is true, yet she goes on to say that black culture is resistance, and she tries to connect styles and behaviors to slavery. "Our style of dress, the extra flair, stems back to the desires of enslaved people—shorn of all individuality—to exert their own identity." I thought the point of this Project was to teach the truth about slavery, of which blacks have been deprived. If that is true, how can today's styles be connected to mannerisms of slaves if we have been deprived of the knowledge?

It goes on like this: hairstyles display the determination of enslaved people, the naming practices are acts of resistance, the songs are the songs of slaves in the fields, our speech and fashion echoes Africa but is not African. This makes absolutely no sense and has nothing to do with slavery or discrimination. As for the "naming practices," she forgot to mention those names are neither European nor American; they are retail products, like beverages and automobiles.

She ends this section with an indictment of white Americans trying to solve the "Negro problem." She says:

> It is common, still, to point to rates of black poverty, out-of-wedlock births, crime and college attendance, as if these conditions in a country built on a racial caste system are not utterly predictable.

Perhaps her Project should shift its focus from complaining about whites to solving that "Negro problem." She claims our greatness comes from slavery, celebrating how we fought and achieved despite debilitating oppression; yet somehow, we cannot make the same efforts against drugs, crime, gangs, lack of fathers, and poor education. If greatness comes from within, from those rising to their challenges, it seems counterproductive to focus on who created the problems rather than how to fix them. Especially if your best argument is that the problem was created 400 years ago.

She closes her essay with another story from her childhood. She was in fifth or sixth grade and was given an assignment to draw the flag of her ancestral land. She felt no tie to a country in Africa and no tie to America. It is great that she says that she should have said her ancestry started here, but I wonder if she means it. She spends the greater part of her essay pointing out America's flaws, and where she says something positive, it is solely about blacks and more a finger in the eyes of whites than it is pride or an expression of a connection to America.

Her essay also suffers from many lies of omission and factual inaccuracies, some of which I mentioned. She started with 1619, for obvious reasons, but never mentioned abolitionists, Radical Republicans, or the decades-long battle to stop the expansion of slavery by many white lawmakers. That is understandable because it does not fit her narrative, but she also excluded Frederick Douglass, Booker T. Washington, or the talent produced at HBCUs. She focused largely on the South, ignoring the fact that the nation's capital and many of its most prominent Founders were not from the states on which her essay was focused.

Her essay is heavily reliant upon pure opinion. This is fine in the confines of the *New York Times Magazine,* but many public schools are promising to use this anti-American, anti-white essay as an educational tool in history and social studies classes across America. The only conclusion one could draw from this essay is that whites are bad, and blacks are great but cannot truly shine because whites are bad. This Project will do more harm than good. It will leave students with a lack of historical knowledge and create bitter, entitled students with a radical hatred of America.

Hannah-Jones does a great job showing past racism, but what is missing are solutions. She does not offer one idea on how to fix the "broken" white people or uplift black Americans. She says that blacks are facing "rampant discrimination." This is patently false. Her Ida B. Wells Society exposes alleged injustices perpetrated by the government. I believe this is a situation where if you spend enough time searching for injustices, you start to see them everywhere. She also hinted at "redress" but never explained what this means.

Finally, this is not the Founders' country. They are to be lauded for setting the stage for us. They started a nation governed by the people, and we are the people—not just the white elites or the blacks Nikole Hannah-Jones speaks of—but all of us. We should be trying to live up to the idea of America rather than working so hard to prove the idea was flawed. America is great and unique in the world, but it cannot stay that way if we allow future generations to be exposed to its reframing by the toxic narrative of The 1619 Project.

13

CAPITALISM

In order to understand the brutality of American capitalism, you have to start on the plantation.
—Matthew Desmond

Building off the crumbled foundation of its founder, Nikole Hannah-Jones, the essays that follow are extensions of her initial presentation. They serve as reflections of her assessment of the country and its treatment of blacks, just condensed to a specific topic. The first of these, "American capitalism is brutal. You can trace that to the plantation," is an explanation of American capitalism and its ties to slavery. It was written by Matthew Desmond, a professor of Sociology at Princeton University.

The essay opens with the story of Martin Shkreli, the former CEO of Turing Pharmaceuticals, who is now in federal prison after being convicted on securities fraud.[100] He was universally condemned for purchasing the rights to Daraprim, a drug that cost $13.50 per pill and raising the price to $756 per pill. He was quoted as saying, "No one wants to say it, no one's proud of it, but this is a capitalist society, a capitalist system, and capitalist rules."

Desmond then states:

> When Americans declare that "we live in a capitalist society," what they're often defending is our nation's peculiarly brutal economy. "Low-road capitalism," the University of Wisconsin-Madison sociologist Joel Rogers has called it. In a capitalist society that goes low, wages are depressed as businesses compete over the price, not the quality, of goods; so-called unskilled workers are typically incentivized through punishments, not promotions; inequality reigns and poverty spreads.

It would be great to have examples of the types of punishment unskilled workers are being subjected to, but they never provide details on dubious accusations like these.

To provide another example, Desmond references a *Miami Herald* interview in which a real estate mogul explained his feelings about small-business owners being evicted from their Little Haiti storefronts. He provided a link but never addressed what he

[100] Dan Mangan, "'Pharma bro' Martin Shkreli found guilty of 3 of 8 charges, including securities fraud," CNBC.com, August 4, 2017. https://www.cnbc.com/2017/08/04/pharma-bro-martin-shkreli-convicted-in-federal-fraud-case.html

said. Here is the context. Desmond was referring to an interview with Jorge Pérez, chairman and CEO of The Related Group, a Miami-based real estate company. In the wide-ranging interview, Pérez was asked his opinion on gentrification; this related to small business owners being displaced by a new landlord.[101]

To summarize his response, Pérez said that there are pros and cons. He understands those who believe that it is bad to evict them, as well as the businessman who buys the property with the hopes of making a profit. Here is what Desmond was likely referencing. Pérez had said, "But we live in a capitalist society that has a rule of law. If you're paying very low rent and you have a short-term lease and somebody comes in and buys that—not just a shop in Little Haiti but anywhere in the U.S.—chances are the landlord is looking to improve the property and maximize income. If we did not have that system, we would be a socialist society."

Desmond believes this type of thinking is discriminatory and immoral. What he does not consider is whether Pérez is correct in his other point about socialism: "Nobody can buy this property, that belongs to the government and we're going to keep the rents at a certain level. What happens if you keep the rents at a certain level? Very simple: You create ghettos." The only alternative for those who argue against capitalism is government control, and everyone knows that is not better. But whatever your views on Shkreli and Pérez, Desmond's point here is clear: Capitalists are greedy and evil, and America is full of them.

---

101 Rene Rodriguez, "Miami condo king Jorge Pérez on gentrification, Liberty Square, and federal investigations," *Miami Herald*, August 6, 2018. https://www.miamiherald.com/news/business/real-estate-news/article215913130.html

Desmond's first method of attack is to create the illusion that capitalism creates poverty. To do this, he makes the claim that the United States has a larger share of working-age people living in poverty than any other country. He includes a link to the Organization for Economic Cooperation and Development's website, where he derived his research.[102] If you click the link, the first thing you notice is that the U.S. does not have the largest share; it is fourth. That is still unusually high, so I am not sure why he felt the need to skew the numbers.

Beyond this oversight, there is a problem with the perception of poverty the essayist is trying to convey. I reviewed Desmond's numbers and discovered the problem; they are not comparing apples to apples. The OECD explains that they calculate each country's poverty rate by taking half of the median household income in that country. The number for each country is expressed in U.S. dollars. At the time of the OECD's reporting, this would make the U.S. poverty line $21,792. This is more than the median household income in 102 of the 131 countries listed. If we made $21,792 the standard to determine poverty across the board, the poverty rate in 125 countries would be greater than 80 percent. Simply put, no American living in poverty would trade places with a middle-class person from Togo, Chad, Georgia, or Tajikistan, all listed above the U.S. based on fuzzy math.

Using income alone is not the best way to assess poverty. To look at poverty honestly, one must include two factors in addition to income: quality of life and opportunity. There is no disputing that the poor in most countries around the world do

[102] "Poverty rate," Organization for Economic Cooperation and Development, data archived at: https://data.oecd.org/inequality/poverty-rate.htm

not enjoy a quality of life equal to that of poor Americans. This leads some to mistakenly call Americans lazy. We are not lazy, we are just used to a level of comfort unique around the world, even for poor people. More importantly, there is no other system and no other place that affords poor people a greater chance to succeed and move up the economic ladder than the U.S. When all is considered, capitalism stacks up pretty well.

Next, Desmond takes on worker rights. He notes that 90 percent of workers in Iceland and 34 percent in Italy belong to trade unions; that number is only 10 percent in the U.S. He is obviously implying that this is not only bad, but it is the fault of capitalism. He ignores the fact that many unions do not offer a product most workers want; they have become highly politicized, and they don't strive for fairness. They strive for sameness, which is not the same thing. He goes on to say that the OECD scores nations on how they regulate temporary work arrangements, and the U.S. ranked last. This is such an esoteric issue that if this is how far he needs to go to show the perils of capitalism, his case is evidently weak.

He describes the American economy as "uniquely severe and unbridled." I have never heard the American economy described in that way. He goes on to say that this is because of cotton houses, the birthplace of low-road capitalism, which started in the Mississippi Valley; and after two average lifetimes, "we can still feel the looming presence of this institution." He continues:

> "American slavery is necessarily imprinted on the DNA of American capitalism," wrote the historians Sven Beckert and Seth Rockman. The task now, they argue, is "cataloging the dominant and recessive traits" that have been passed

> down to us, tracing the unsettling and often unrecognized lines of descent by which America's national sin is now being visited upon the third and fourth generations.

Desmond is obviously continuing Hannah-Jones's talk of the indelible presence of slavery, but they are struggling to connect the dots. He spends much of the rest of the essay using the example of the cotton industry, its growth, how it was managed, and how it was financed to depict capitalism in America as uniquely flawed—different from capitalism anywhere else and wholly dependent upon slavery. "The Mississippi Valley was home to more millionaires per capita than anywhere else in the United States." Desmond wrongly assumes that this could not have happened without slavery—a point later refuted by one of the Project's other contributors.

He goes into detail and uses graphic imagery of the violence of slavery, but none of this changes the fact that capitalism did not enslave anyone; immoral people did. Those slave owners got rich because they had buyers. None of their efforts would work if everyone had refused to buy their tainted goods. Instead, people bought despite how the products were produced. Many would argue this makes those individuals and companies complicit in slavery. That is a fair claim, but the same could be said about the consumers of today.

We buy oil from the Middle East knowing how they treat Christians and gays. The social justice warriors who march daily demanding justice wear Nike products made in sweat shops and Apple watches assembled by child labor. Those early traders, bankers, textile mill operators, shippers, retailers, and many others were doing the same thing. This is human nature, not capitalism, and it is not unique to America. Desmond tries to argue that many investors were unaware of what their money subsidized. Those businessmen knew then, and consumers know today. Capitalism, like any other form of economy, cannot be held to account for the greed, desperation, or indifference of people.

Throughout his essay, there are shorter vignettes looking at more granular issues. The first one is by Mehrsa Baradaran, titled "The Limits of Banking Regulation." She argues, in the same simplistic fashion they all take, that the lack of adequate banking regulation is a result of slavery. Her argument is simple: The National Currency Act of 1863 was created to finance the war; it also created the Office of the Comptroller of the Currency, which allowed the subprime lending crisis to continue. Hence, it all starts with slavery. She writes, "Only the United States has such a fragmentary, overlapping and inefficient system—a direct relic of the conflict between federal and state power over maintenance of the slave-based economy of the South."

Desmond goes on to describe more financial and economic wonders that evolved from slavery. The boom in cotton production necessitated a better way to process the raw material, which hastened the invention of the factory. This propelled the Industrial Revolution. America was developing into a capitalist economy, all due to slavery. He explains:

> Perhaps you are reading this at work, maybe at a multinational corporation that runs like a soft-purring engine. You report to someone, and someone reports to you. Everything is tracked, recorded and analyzed, via vertical reporting systems, double-entry record-keeping and precise quantification. Data seems to hold sway

> over every operation. It feels like a cutting-edge approach to management, but many of these techniques that we now take for granted were developed by and for large plantations.

Was accounting invented out of slavery? Desmond comes close to suggesting this. He writes, "When an accountant depreciates an asset to save on taxes or when a midlevel manager spends an afternoon filling in rows and columns on an Excel spreadsheet, they are repeating business procedures whose roots twist back to slave-labor camps." We are to believe that no one understood expenses and revenues prior to slavery and, but for slavery, no one would have developed it. Slavery even led to a development in the calculation of depreciation. Plantation owners assessed the value of slaves over their lifespans. This did not begin with chattel slavery. People have been valued and devalued since antiquity; that someone put the practice in a book does not make it unique.

Here, Baradaran enters with her second article, "Fiat Currency and the Civil War." Her argument here is that Lincoln needed funding for the war, so he issued the first national currency, tied to U.S. Treasury faith and credit rather than the gold standard. So, in essence, slavery brought about the advent of national currency. For the purposes of analyzing The 1619 Project, there is no sense in debating monetary policy. The key takeaway here is that even when the side that was trying to end slavery creates something, for the purposes of the Project's writers, they consider it "born out of slavery." Also, Baradaran describes the economy of the North as "trade-based." They had a thriving economy; in fact, they were the center of finance, government, culture, and so on. Could it be, then, that the writer's exclusive focus on cotton and the South is inadequate as an examination of the capitalism in America?

Desmond then makes his attempt the connect today's business leaders to the plantation owners. He writes:

> Today modern technology has facilitated unremitting workplace supervision, particularly in the service sector. Companies have developed software that records workers' keystrokes and mouse clicks, along with randomly capturing screenshots multiple times a day. Modern-day workers are subjected to a wide variety of surveillance strategies, from drug tests and closed-circuit video monitoring to tracking apps and even devices that sense heat and motion. A 2006 survey found that more than a third of companies with work forces of 1,000 or more had staff members who read through employees' outbound emails. The technology that accompanies this workplace supervision can make it feel futuristic. But it is only the technology that is new. The core impulse behind that technology pervaded plantations, which sought innermost control over the bodies of their enslaved work force.

Now the connection is clear. Multinational corporations are plantations, and Jeff Bezos, Elon Musk, and the American capitalists are modern-day cotton barons. Based on Desmond's assessment of how the American economy was wholly predicated on slavery, it would be interesting to hear his explanation of how the North survived, since they had been slave-free for more than sixty years by the start of the Civil War. He would have you believe American businessmen were so innovative and forward-thinking, yet they would never have found a way to thrive without slave labor.

He goes on to discuss slavery's effects on poor whites. He rightly points out that slavery drove down wages, but he compares it to the plight of day laborers today, when the better comparison would be the day laborer driving down wages of unskilled Americans. Slaves were being abused, while day laborers choose to do the work, even if they are being exploited for their lack of legal status. Slavery was also used to limit complaints from poor whites, giving them a graphic example that things could be worse. This should serve as a celebration of capitalism rather than a rebuke. Without the morally repugnant institution of slavery, capitalism would have done what it was designed to do.

There is one quote of Desmond's I found particularly interesting. In pointing out that slavery is complex, he writes:

> There is some comfort, I think, in attributing the sheer brutality of slavery to dumb racism. It was not so much the rage of the poor white Southerner but the greed of the rich white planter that drove the lash. The violence was neither arbitrary nor gratuitous. It was rational, capitalistic, all part of the plantation's design.

This is a rare use of context in these discussions and in direct contradiction to Hannah-Jones's assertion that everything bad in America can be traced to anti-black racism. Of course, he goes on to blame it on capitalism, so his argument is still flawed.

He then expresses problems with the financialization of the American economy. He argues that the repeal of Glass–Steagall led to a boon of interest rates, creating new streams of revenue for the wealthy at the expense of poorer Americans; this unfair practice, which increased the wealth gap, began during slavery.

The third of Baradaran's articles, "Cotton and the Global Market," leads directly to Desmond's next section. She talks of futures trading, common law standards, and ways for traders to mitigate risk, all coming from slavery. Desmond describes all of this as the evils of American capitalism, but even he cannot escape the fact that capitalism does not have a national identity. As Baradaran points out, this is a global market, and none of this economic explosion is possible without global participation.

Desmond notes that when Thomas Jefferson mortgaged his slaves, a Dutch firm put up the money. Additionally, the Louisiana Purchase was financed by Baring Brothers, a British commercial bank. To raise capital, state banks sold bonds to Germany and the Netherlands. Yet, we are supposed to ignore these global transactions or assume these foreign businesses did not know about the slaves suffering in America. Surprisingly, Desmond floated that argument. Basically, these countries were moral until America corrupted them with slavery money.

He discusses how slaveowners used their enslaved workers as financial collateral. This, he argues, is how many Americans were first exposed to the concept of a mortgage. This is a curious claim, as most of the colonists, and their descendants, were Christians who were avid Bible readers. The Bible states in Nehemiah 5:3, "We have *mortgaged* our lands, vineyards, and houses, that we might buy corn, because of dearth." This was written as early as 400 B.C.E., yet we are to believe that the mortgage was a product of slavery in America.

In the last article, Tiya Miles steps in as guest writer with her summary of "How Slavery Made Wall Street." Again, by her account, all the signs point to America, even though she admits that its building was started by the Dutch and finished by the English Duke of York, who defeated the Dutch to gain control. She goes on to correctly state that bankers and financiers profited from slavery. This adds nothing to the essay as it has already been established that financiers all over the world did this. As evil and wrong as it was, it was ubiquitous, so mentioning it does not prove a point and singling out America is deceptive.

The essay ends with the collapse of the cotton market. Desmond blames this on capitalism and draws parallels to the stock market crash of 2008. He believes the speculation on cotton is similar to that of the housing market. This is an oversimplification of both issues, but it is also a mischaracterization of capitalism.

Capitalism is an economic system characterized by private or corporate ownership of capital goods, by investments that are determined by private decision, and by prices, production, and the distribution of goods that are determined mainly by competition in a free market. This says nothing about slavery or futures markets. Financial instruments have expanded exponentially over the last century, but whatever your beliefs are of the current financial system, it should not be used to indict capitalism.

Let us return to the previous example of segregated streetcars. According to Roback, several streetcar operators were against segregation and not because of their openness to blacks. The reason they most often gave was that separate cars and sections would be too expensive.[103] This shows how capitalism would have risen above racism if not for government intervention. Despite the owners' beliefs on race, true capitalists would have taken money from all customers.

In his economic theory of discrimination, Gary Becker goes further. He defines "tastes of discrimination" as a willingness to pay to avoid contact with the other race.[104] He argues that absent segregation laws, whites who did not want to sit next to blacks would be willing to pay more to sit in cars that were "exclusively white," creating segregation for those who desired it without the need of a law. The point here is that racism caused the problem and, left to its own devices, capitalism would have solved it.

Condemning capitalism is short-sighted. What The 1619 Project is saying is that slavery, greed, and other immoral practices prove that capitalism does not work. By that logic, socialism, communism, egalitarianism, and every economic and philosophical "ism" work without bad behavior. The writers proceed as if evil practices did not exist prior to capitalism or that capitalism cannot exist without them. We know the fallacy of the former, and we are proof of the latter.

After slavery, the Mississippi Valley millionaires Desmond spoke of lost their wealth, but the country got richer. Most plantation owners lost their land, either due to destruction during the war, insurmountable debt, or an inability to adequately maintain the land without forced laborers. Capitalists then came in and

---

103 Jennifer Roback, "The political economy of segregation: The case of segregated streetcars," *The Journal of Economic History,* Vol. XLVI, No. 4, December 1986, pp. 893-917. https://www.jstor.org/stable/2121814

104 Gary S. Becker, *The Economies of Discrimination* (2nd ed., Chicago, 1973).

bought this land for pennies on the dollar. American capitalism had no sympathy for these former slaveholders. The system allowed blacks to buy plots, philanthropists to open schools, and gave the South an opportunity to rebuild its economy. President Grant balanced the budget, the Industrial Revolution catapulted the U.S. to superpower status, and America went on to build companies and develop technologies that modernized the world. This was all done without slaves but with the help of capitalism.

14

A Broken Healthcare System

Why doesn't the United States have universal health care? The answer has everything to do with race.
—Jeneen Interlandi

Jeneen Interlandi, a member of *The New York Times's* editorial board and a staff writer for the magazine, pens this essay, "Why Doesn't America Have Universal Healthcare? One Word: Race." As her quotation at the opening of this chapter suggests, she aims to explain how opposition to universal healthcare stems from slavery.

The essay opens with a smallpox outbreak in the United States after the Civil War. African-American communities were hit hardest by the disease. There is no implication here that blacks were intentionally sickened or that whites wanted blacks to die, yet there was greater concern for keeping the virus out of white communities than there was for mitigating the epidemic in black communities. She quotes historian Jim Downs from his book *Sick from Freedom*:

> They worried about black epidemics spilling into their own communities and wanted the formerly enslaved to be healthy enough to return to plantation work. But they also feared that free and healthy African-Americans would upend the racial hierarchy.

When the government did act, they did not do enough. The medical division of the Freedmen's Bureau was established to address the health crisis but did not deploy enough doctors or supply them with the necessary equipment. Newly erected hospitals were prematurely shuttered. Interlandi continues:

> One of the most eloquent rejoinders to the theory of black extinction came from Rebecca Lee Crumpler, the nation's first black female doctor. Crumpler was born free and trained and practiced in Boston. At the close of the war, she joined the Freedmen's Bureau and worked in the freed people's communities of Virginia. In 1883, she published one of the first treatises on the burden of disease in black communities. "They seem to forget there is a cause for every ailment," she wrote. "And that it may be in their power to remove it."

During Reconstruction, the Democrats created a powerful, uniformly segregationist voting bloc. They held power for decades and used the "states' rights" argument to dictate how programs were implemented, most commonly with discriminatory intent. This continued into the 1930s and 1940s as many blacks were excluded from New Deal policies, including Social Security, the eight-hour workday, the minimum wage, and the G.I. Bill, to name a few. When the federal government provided grants for states to build hospitals in communities of need, the states controlled the funding and segregated the facilities.

This portion of the essay lays the foundation for what is to come. It is mostly factual and highlights many obviously racist practices. Some of it was added to drive home the fact that intentional discrimination was endemic in America for decades; but it had little if anything to do with healthcare.

Interlandi highlights the tremendous work blacks did to improve the health of their communities despite the discrimination they faced. They educated people, raised funds for black healthcare facilities, and created programs to bring national attention to the problem of healthcare inequalities in the black community. Black doctors and nurses started their own professional organizations. They began pushing for a federal healthcare system.

Here is where Interlandi changes her approach. She argues that, as in the present-day debates, those who fought against the national plan used a "vitriolic campaign," calling the idea socialist. We are all free to our own opinion but not our own facts. Regardless of whether you are for or against universal healthcare, the label is not vitriolic; it is accurate. Wanting an entire industry to be controlled by the government is at least socialist, and more accurately communist. Either way, she never connects her argument to slavery.

She is making the claim that the socialist label used in the 1930s and 1940s was a cover for racism and argues that the rebuke of universal healthcare today is the same; it is not. This essay is a political advertisement disguised as an exploration of racial bias. If you have not been convinced of this, here is a quote from the essay that will make it clear. "Several states, most of them in the former Confederacy, refused to participate in Medicaid expansion." Why mention the former Confederacy?

Interlandi performs the bait and switch that every good universal healthcare advocate does. Her entire essay is about people, mostly blacks, being denied *care*. When she changes her discussion to 2010, the conversation changed to health *insurance*. This is not an oversight or immaterial. When she spoke of denied care and segregation, most visualized a situation like a black man being taken to a "white" hospital and being refused treatment. That is true denial of care. This does not exist in America; people who need life-saving care get it regardless of their ability to pay.

There is a place for the debate over universal health insurance. Proponents say that it would improve the health of the nation by ensuring everyone has access. They also believe it will result in better overall healthcare. Opponents see nothing but exponentially higher taxes and another overburdened system run by bureaucrats. Whatever side of the argument you come down on, the argument should not be predicated on race.

Interlandi spends much of her essay explaining how the government intentionally discriminated against blacks. The discrimination and racism were widespread, including doctors, the American Medical Association, state legislators, congressmen, and many more. Yet now she implies that a healthcare system controlled by these same organizations is the solution to all racial disparities.

She began the essay using the example of smallpox. As I write this, the country is grappling with the coronavirus. There has been outrage and widespread criticism of the government's reaction. Some say that the government went too far with restrictions; others say they waited too long and did not go far enough. Most saw partisan division and argued along party lines. What I saw was government in action. Now, at the height of a global crisis, many await a return to normalcy. With all the uncertainty, one thing is abundantly clear: we would still be waiting for a vaccine if it had to come from the government.

— 15 —

Traffic

What does a traffic jam in Atlanta have to do with segregation? Quite a lot.
—Kevin M. Kruse

Kevin Kruse, professor of history at Princeton University, opens his essay, "How Segregation Caused Your Traffic Jam," by describing the gridlock that permeates Atlanta traffic. But his goal is really to highlight the issues of urban planning and how it is used to control and segregate people. This is no revelation. Everyone knows that segregation exists today, has long been in effect, and is largely believed to be a product of racism. So, what is Kruse trying to teach us? Consistent with the Project's mission, he is trying to link beliefs during slavery to the segregation we see today. I will concede that much of what he writes is true, yet, as we continue to see, what is left out is often critical to understanding similarities and differences from the past.

After highlighting the traffic problem and explaining that it was by design, Kruse makes his obligatory connection to slavery. He does this by randomly inserting a fact that does not connect to his essay. He writes, "Before the Civil War, white masters kept enslaved African-Americans close at hand to coerce their labor and guard against revolts. But with the abolition of slavery, the spatial relationship was reversed. Once they had no need to keep constant watch over African-Americans, whites wanted them out of sight." In summary, the slavery connection is that segregation started after slavery.

Next, he correctly points out that there were overt laws mandating segregation. That, coupled with terrorism by the Klan, kept the races apart. This is key, because as racist as the motives for segregation were, this presents a flaw in Kruse's argument. The point of his essay is that racist government officials used the interstate to segregate the races, yet according to his own timeline, the races were already segregated. It does not mean they did not want the races segregated; it means they did not need a highway to do it. He writes as though these urban areas were integrated, then the interstate pried the races apart—or as if he believes that if the interstate did not exist, segregation would have summarily ended.

My mom grew up in Gary, Indiana. The city was segregated her entire childhood, and she graduated high school before there was an interstate. People in smaller towns talked about growing up on "the wrong side of the tracks." The point here is that there has always been a delineation to separate classes or races of people. The interstate may have continued segregation, but it did not create it. And it can be argued that segregation was not the primary reason for it.

Many cities were grappling with growth and looking for ways to maximize the economy and garner increased investment. Kruse argues that interstates regularly destroyed black neighborhoods. This is true, but he ignores the intersection of race and class. He notes local expressways and interstates were steered along routes that bulldozed "blighted" neighborhoods that housed the poorest residents. I have no doubt that the state and local leaders managing the development had little concern for their black residents, but shouldn't the "blighted" aspect be highlighted? Does anyone think that they would have bulldozed an affluent neighborhood? When searching for land for a new development, they always start with poorer neighborhoods.

When looking for a racist angle, one can always find one, but reviewing the facts with the sole goal of understanding the truth provides clearer context. As Steven Malanga writes in his *City Journal* article, "Racist Interstates?", a largely Jewish community was displaced to build the Cross Bronx Expressway as were thousands of residents and hundreds of businesses in Boston's largely Italian-American north end to build Boston's Central Artery.[105] Bad public policy doesn't have to be the result of racism.

Kruse suggests that the solution to easing the traffic woes is mass transit, but the Metropolitan Atlanta Rapid Transit Authority (MARTA) is continually rejected by the residents of majority-white counties. There are several examples that his attempt to imply this is solely about race are unfounded. One example is his label of Cobb County as "nearly all-white." It is not appropriate to describe a county with 30 percent minority residents as nearly all-white. He also deceptively mentioned

[105] Steven Malanga, "Racist interstates?" *City Journal*, Autumn 2020. https://www.city-journal.org/revamping-interstates-based-on-racial-equity

Gwinnett and Clayton counties voting down the MARTA in 1971. What he does not tell you is that Gwinnett is now less than 50 percent white, and Clayton is majority-black. The 1971 vote is fifty years old and was only used to push a racist narrative.

He continues by highlighting forty-year-old racist comments and unfounded racial assumptions. He quotes the white chairman of MARTA—his description, not mine—insisting that suburban opposition to mass transit had been "90 percent a racial issue." He has no way of knowing this, and 90 percent is highly unlikely. He did admit that as the suburbs became more racially diverse, they remained opposed to MARTA. Yet, he only quotes white people rather than trying to determine why minority suburbanites would also vote against the project.

Kruse also ignores obvious nuances in segregation. We all assume that segregation is always bad and always racist. What does this say about people who desire to live among a group with whom they feel a connection? As a black man, I know many people who prefer to live in majority-black communities. No one calls this racist, but based on our common assumptions, it is. Recently there was a story of nineteen black families who purchased ninety acres of land in Georgia as a "safe space for black people."[106] White liberals celebrated this. Isn't this to be considered racist?

The last point I would like to mention in relation to segregation is gentrification. It is surprising that Kruse would write an essay about segregation and omit it. In recent years, this has

---

[106] Pamela Kirkland, "19 families buy nearly 97 acres of land in Georgia to create a city safe for Black people," CNN.com, September 12, 2020. https://www.cnn.com/2020/09/12/us/freedom-black-cooperative-toomsboro/index.html

become a widely debated topic. Many blacks and white liberals argue against gentrification. They claim that whites moving into urban areas displace many of the lower-income blacks who live there. There is truth to this, but no one addresses what this argument means. Keeping neighborhoods black is basically arguing *for* segregation. These are the same people who once championed integration and today want to destroy the suburbs.[107] It seems racist to say blacks can live wherever they want, but whites cannot.

Locking people out of areas and using race as a determinant to dictate resources or urban planning is wrong, and there is no doubt that this was done deliberately in the past. However, using decades-old quotations and ignoring demographic trends to tie those racist practices of the past to the city's current situation provides little insight into the complexities of the problem and gives no path for improvement.

---

[107] Stanley Kurtz, "Biden and Dems are set to abolish the suburbs," *National Review*, June 30, 2020. https://www.nationalreview.com/corner/biden-and-dems-are-set-to-abolish-the-suburbs/

16

Undemocratic Democracy

America holds onto an undemocratic assumption from its founding: that some people deserve more power than others.
—Jamelle Bouie

It is 2011, and everyone in Washington is concerned about the debt ceiling. We have reached our limit, and the Democrats are calling for an increase, but Congressional Republicans have a different idea. With their new control, having won back the House in 2010, they planned to flex their muscles. At a closed-door retreat, days before the session began, the *Washington Post* reports Majority Leader Eric Cantor saying, "I'm asking you to look at a potential increase in the debt limit as a leverage moment when the White House and President Obama will have to deal with us."[108]

For many, this is seen as politics as usual; Jamelle Bouie, *New York Times* columnist and former chief correspondent for Slate magazine describes it as "reactionary extremism" in his essay, "What the Reactionary Politics of 2019 Owe to the Politics of Slavery."

He uses this term to describe the Republican Party and accuses the American voters of electing them as a "backlash to Obama's Presidency." Who were these voters who were so offended by an Obama presidency that they elected Republican congressmen and senators, then elected Obama for a second term two years later? Some would have you believe this was just rural Americans in Red States, but the Republicans enjoyed a net gain of sixty-three seats all over the country. If this were Obama fatigue or outrage, he surely would have lost in 2012.

Bouie goes on to call the Tea Party Republicans "insurgents" and describes Senate Republican Leader Mitch McConnell's tactics as effectively nullifying the president's ability to nominate federal judges and fill vacancies in the executive branch. McConnell would become the Leader of the Senate in 2014, blocking the president's Supreme Court nominee. Bouie asks, "Where did this destructive, sectarian style of partisan politics come from?" This is an important description to remember. He continues with some of their "destructive" actions.

---

[108] Brady Dennis, Alec MacGillis, and Lori Montgomery, "Origins of the debt showdown," *The Washington Post*, August 6, 2011. https://www.washingtonpost.com/business/economy/origins-of-the-debt-showdown/2011/08/03/gIQA9uqIzI_story.html

Republicans took the position of total opposition, not just blocking Obama but also casting him as fundamentally illegitimate and un-American. They took the House hostage. "Republicans would either win total victory or they would wreck the system itself." Keep in mind this essay was written in 2019. It would be interesting to track Bouie down for comment. Everything he has described can be applied to Nancy Pelosi's tenure as Speaker of the House, and there is no doubt that if the Democrats controlled the Senate, President Trump would meet the same fate.

Bouie uses South Carolina as his link to the sectarian Republicans of the 112th Congress. In the early nineteenth century, rich slaveowners controlled the state, but this could not compensate for declining national politics. The North was gaining power and making progress toward ending slavery. The slaveowners wanted to protect what they thought was their right, and their greatest asset was John C. Calhoun.

John Calhoun was the most prominent politician of his time. Though he failed in his many presidential runs, he was a master negotiator and one of the most effective diplomats and senators. He was also an open advocate of slavery among elected officials. He argued that slavery was a positive good. He was also one of the most ardent supporters of states' rights. Bouie honestly assesses him, except he slyly describes him as "an influence on 'right-wing' thinking." I know many "right-wing" thinkers and have never heard any of them quote Calhoun or mention him in a positive light.

This is a mischaracterization of the argument of states' rights. The issue of states' rights is not "right-wing" thinking; it is in the constitution. Article I, Sections VIII through X, list the powers given to Congress, the limits on that power, and the powers prohibited of the states. After clearly establishing this, the Tenth Amendment states, "The powers not delegated to the United States by the Constitution, nor prohibited by it to the States, are reserved to the States respectively, or to the people." This means most rights remain with the states.

Standing up for those rights has nothing to do with nullification. Nullification means that a state does not have to follow any federal law it deems unconstitutional. What a state deems means nothing. If the law is consistent with Article I of the Constitution, the states must follow it, and that would be for courts to decide. Nullification is just a theory since it has never been argued in court, and no twenty-first-century Republican has taken up its cause. This is just a red herring used to imply that Republicans want some votes to have more weight than others. The 1619 authors cannot find evidence to support that claim.

Tiya Miles adds an article arguing, "How Slavery Made Its Way West." She explains how the desire for more fertile land to expand the cotton industry was the catalyst for the theft of Native American lands and their subsequent removal to "Indian Territory" by President Andrew Jackson. Because of this aggressive expansion, the first blacks in the West were brought as property. Though the Western states outlawed slavery, most settlers kept their slaves until after the Civil War. While Miles's article consists of interesting information, it has nothing to do with democracy.

Bouie then tries to resurrect Calhoun's ghost by saying that when Northern Democrats added a civil rights plank to their party platform, thirty-five delegates from Mississippi and Alabama walked out in protest. This, he claims, was the prologue to the "Dixiecrat revolt"—their eventual shift to the Republican party. There was no wholesale switch, but this myth is so ingrained it would take an entire essay to debunk. I would simply suggest that anyone who believes it check the voting percentages in the South, by race and gender, from 1930 through 1980.

Calhoun is back lending his ideas to the resistance of the *Brown v. Board of Education* decision, then hands the baton to William F. Buckley, the founding editor of the *National Review*. Bouie includes a quotation of Buckley's from a 1957 article he wrote amid debate over the first Civil Rights Act. Buckley wrote:

> Is whether the white community in the South is entitled to take such measures as are necessary to prevail, politically and culturally, in areas which it does not predominate numerically? The sobering answer is yes—the white community is so entitled because, for the time being, it is the advanced race.... It is more important for any community, anywhere in the world, to affirm and live by civilized standards, than to bow to the demands of the numerical majority.

This is clearly racist, but it does not comport with most of the writing and videos I have seen of Buckley, and the "for the time being" struck me as odd, so I searched for some context. I found a *Politico* article titled, "How William F. Buckley Jr. Changed His Mind on Civil Rights." In the article, they continue from his 1957 op-ed:

> In the same op-ed, Buckley concluded that as long as African-Americans remained "backward" in education and in economic progress, Southern whites had a right to "impose superior

> mores for whatever period it takes to affect a genuine cultural equality between the races." In defense of his position that whites, for the time being, remained the "more advanced race," Buckley pointed to the name a major civil rights organization, The National Association for the Advancement of Colored People had adopted for itself as evidence that its founders considered its constituents "less advanced." The remainder of his comments are still racist, but they are less John C. Calhoun and more 21st century white liberal woman.[109]

In his efforts to prove states' rights are bad, and all its proponents are racist, Bouie continued the often-repeated libel of Barry Goldwater. Barry Goldwater was an Arizona Senator and the 1964 Republican presidential nominee. He was indeed a states' rights advocate, but Bouie describes him as an opponent of the Civil Rights Act and thereby an opponent of the demands of the black-freedom movement. Nothing could be further from the truth.

First and foremost, Goldwater was not an opponent of black freedom. He fought for equal rights and desegregation in Arizona even before it was approved federally. He was a member of the NAACP and Urban League in Arizona and supported the Urban League financially for years. In 1991, he received a humanitarian award for "50 years of loyal service to the Phoenix Urban

[109] Alvin Felzenberg, "How William F. Buckley, Jr., changed his mind on civil rights," *Politico*, May 13, 2017. https://www.politico.com/magazine/story/2017/05/13/william-f-buckley-civil-rights-215129

League."[110] As for his vote on the Civil Rights Act of 1964, he voted against it because he felt two titles in the act were unconstitutional.

Bouie moves on from his states' rights attack and devolves into the left's stale argument that conservatives simply want to preserve a white America and limit minorities. He includes a quote from Samuel Francis, a polemicist who would eventually migrate to the "very far right" of American conservatism. This is how Francis identified this dynamic in the context of David Duke's campaign for governor of Louisiana:

> Reagan conservatism, in its innermost meaning, had little to do with supply-side economics and spreading democracy. It had to do with the awakening of a people who face political, cultural and economic dispossession, who are slowly beginning to glimpse the fact of dispossession and what dispossession will mean for them and their descendants, and who also are starting to think about reversing the processes and powers responsible for their dispossession.

Why include a quote in the context of a Klan member running for office, from an open, white supremacist, to describe what Reagan conservatism meant four decades ago? It screams of bias and it adds nothing. It is not as if Francis is quoting Reagan. Bouie continues with the same attack on the Tea Party:

---

110 Lee Edwards, "In Barry Goldwater, the conscience of a conservative," *Miami Herald*, July 2, 2014. https://www.miamiherald.com/article1973798.html

> The past 10 years of Republican extremism is emblematic. The Tea Party billed itself as a reaction to debt and spending, but a close look shows it was actually a reaction to an ascendant majority of black people, Latinos, Asian-Americans, and liberal white people. In their survey-based study of the movement, the political scientists Christopher S. Parker and Matt A. Barreto show that Tea Party Republicans were motivated "by the fear and anxiety associated with the perception that 'real' Americans are losing their country."

The Tea Party started out of concerns over taxation and spending. It was literally called the Taxed Enough Already Party. This is evidenced by the fact that it started under George W. Bush, and the group only addressed those issues. If this is how Bouie sees the Tea Party, I would hate to see his scathing description of the Black Lives Matter movement. Keep in mind, Tea Party rallies never ended with broken windows, shootings, or random acts of violence.

In 2012, Bouie writes, North Carolina Republicans won legislative and executive power for the first time in more than a century. They used it to gerrymander the electoral map and impose new restrictions on voting, specifically aimed at the state's African-American voters. There are three problems with this statement. The first challenges his earlier assertion that Southerners switched to the Republican Party. North Carolina was a Southern stronghold, and here Bouie admits the state had been run by Democrats for over one hundred years. Next, he has no way of knowing why the Republicans redistricted. Finally, Democrats gerrymander, too.

The problem of gerrymandering is all about power.[111] Generally, it is used to help the incumbent, regardless of party. Bouie mentioned Wisconsin and Michigan as further examples of Republican gerrymandering but neglected to mention California, Illinois, and Maryland. Republicans were also accused of trying to draw black voters into two districts. If this is wrong, the same should be said for Democrats in California and Illinois who drew districts to create strong black and Hispanic districts. It is disingenuous to imply it is just a Republican practice.

Bouie then makes the wild assertion that President Trump denounced Hillary Clinton's popular vote victory because he believes that a majority made up of liberals and people of color is not a real majority. This, while including the president's reasoning in his own words. "I won the popular vote if you deduct the millions of people who voted illegally." While his assertion is unfounded, he has no way of knowing how many people voted illegally, and it is certainly not millions of people; it is clear he is talking about illegitimate votes, not people. Taking his statement to mean "people of color" is race-baiting.

Bouie continues his racial gymnastics by stating that:

> The recent attempt to place a citizenship question on the census was an important part of this effort. By asking for this information, the

[111] Alice Li, Jayne Orenstein, and Dan Balz, "Gerrymandering in California: Where do you draw the lines?," *Washington Post*, June 18, 2018. https://www.washingtonpost.com/graphics/2018/national/gerrymandering-in-california-where-do-you-draw-the-lines/

> administration would suppress the number of immigrant respondents, worsening their representation in the House and the Electoral College, reweighting power to the white, rural areas that back the president and the Republican Party.

Immigrants are not here illegally, and the left deliberately conflate them with illegal immigrants. The country has a growing number of people who came here illegally, and we have no accurate account for them. The federal government has an obligation to follow the Constitution and follow the law. If the left wants to change laws concerning people here illegally, they need to win the debate and change the laws. It should not be considered racist to enforce the laws. Unfortunately, these types of arguments are used to create racial animosity and fear, usually among blacks who are most likely to be hurt by the influx of undocumented workers and their drain on the system.

Here is how Bouie closes the essay:

> You could make the case that none of this has anything to do with slavery and slaveholder ideology. You could argue that it has nothing to do with race at all, that it is simply an aggressive effort to secure conservative victories. But the tenor of an argument, the shape and nature of an opposition movement—these things matter. The goals may be colorblind, but the methods of action—the attacks on the legitimacy of nonwhite political actors, the casting of rival political majorities as unrepresentative, the drive to nullify democratically elected governing

> coalitions—are clearly downstream of a style of extreme political combat that came to fruition in the defense of human bondage.

He basically concedes the fact that there is no evidence of racism. However, he *feels* conservatives are racist, so their political victories are racist. In addition, he is arguing that weakening their opponents is weakening democracy. This is not true, and I do not believe he means it. If democracy is truly his concern, I would expect him to admonish the Democrats for obstructing the president.

Finally, he accuses Republicans of attacking "non-white" political actors; aren't Hillary Clinton, Joe Biden, and Nancy Pelosi white political actors, whom they also attack? This argument is as desperate as the attempt to link everything to slavery.

17

Medical Inequality

Myths about physical racial differences were used to justify slavery—and are still believed by doctors today.
—Linda Villarosa

In this essay, "How False Beliefs in Physical Racial Difference Still Live in Medicine Today"," we are given a detailed account of the torture experienced by a former slave named John Brown. Brown would eventually escape to England and recount his story in his autobiography, *Slave Life in Georgia: A Narrative of the Life, Sufferings, and Escape of John Brown, a Fugitive Slave, Now in England.* His abuse was at the hands of Dr. Thomas Hamilton, a respected physician and plantation owner. Hamilton believed that there were physical differences between blacks and whites and experimented on Brown, and others, to confirm his beliefs.

The essayist here, Linda Villarosa, author and former executive editor of *Essence* magazine, highlights the two most persistent medical myths about blacks: higher pain thresholds, and weaker lungs.

She references a 1787 manual by Dr. Benjamin Moseley, a British doctor who claimed that black people could bear the pains of surgical operations much more than whites. Moseley noted, "What would be the cause of insupportable pain to a white man, a Negro would almost disregard." To drive home his point, he added, "I have amputated the legs of many Negroes who have held the upper part of the limb themselves." Another doctor, J. Marion Sims, performed procedures on enslaved women to perfect a surgical technique to repair vesicovaginal fistula, which can be an extreme complication of childbirth.

Villarosa introduces us to Samuel Cartwright, a physician and professor at the University of Louisiana. He was a supposed expert on "diseases of the Negro" and his claims were widely believed. His paper, "Report on the Diseases and Physical Peculiarities of the Negro Race," argued that blacks had lower lung capacity, and forced labor was a way to correct the problem. He also claimed that slaves were prone to a "disease of the mind" called drapetomania, which caused them to run away. He prescribed "whipping the devil out of them" as a preventative measure.

Here is where the first link is made to today's medical beliefs. Dr. Cartwright was one of the first doctors in the United States to measure pulmonary function using a spirometer. He calculated the deficiency in blacks at 20 percent. Today, Villarosa notes, most commercially available spirometers have a "race correction" built into the software.

I am not a doctor, and to a layman this seems blatantly racist, possibly even evidence of malpractice. But my logical thinking leads me to two obvious questions. The first is, is it true? Beliefs that there are intellectual or developmental differences between the races are false, yet there are medical conditions that are more prevalent within certain ethnic groups. Second, if it is not true, why is this allowed? If there is no difference in lung capacity between blacks and whites, one would assume that the race correction in the machines would lead to incorrect diagnoses. The discrepancy in the machine is widely known, and medical students are still taught the racial differences according to Lundy Braun, a Brown University professor of medical science and Africana studies, yet myriad black doctors, business leaders, scientists, professors, politicians, and journalists allow it to continue. There is likely an explanation, but Villarosa does not bother to address it.

Villarosa next addressed a 2013 study that shows racial disparities in pain management. According to her, the study shows black and Hispanic people, from children to elders in hospice care, received inadequate pain management compared to whites. It seems there is truth to the argument that blacks are more likely to have their pain undermedicated. Those who follow race-focused theories view findings such as these as evidence of racism, yet the results are usually more complex. Here are the results of the study detailing racial influences:[112]

- African Americans were found to have lower pain thresholds than whites for cold, heat, pressure, and ischemia.
- Most studies showed no racial differences in pain intensity ratings.

[112] Ronald Wyatt, "Pain and ethnicity," *AMA Journal of Ethics*, May 2013. https://journalofethics.ama-assn.org/article/pain-and-ethnicity/2013-05

- African Americans were more likely than non-Hispanic whites to underreport pain and unpleasantness in the clinical setting, especially in the presence of physicians who were perceived as having "higher social status."
- African Americans were more likely to attribute pain to personal inadequacies and to use "passive" coping strategies, such as prayer, than were non-Hispanic whites.

While there is evidence that some of the disparities are likely due to racial misconceptions, it is not the sole determinant. Perhaps having a better cultural understanding of blacks would be beneficial in minimizing these discrepancies, but labeling doctors as racist because blacks are underreporting their pain is not helpful.

Villarosa follows this with a 2016 study showing that an alarming percentage of medical students and residents, half according to her essay, believed at least one physiological myth about blacks. This is the same study I referenced back in the chapter on the Movement for Black Lives's war on black health. According to Villarosa, one-third of the medical students and residents surveyed believed that black skin is thicker than white skin. This is another mischaracterization of the data. It is important to get this right because if doctors get it wrong, black lives are at stake. Fifty percent would not demand better training, it would confirm systemic racism, and immediate action would be necessary. A deeper look at the numbers suggests a more manageable problem.

First, the respondents were not doctors: They were medical students and residents. To her credit, Villarosa did include this in the essay, but she also included the question about nerve endings, which implied the medical students believed this. The actual average response to the nerve-ending myth, by medical students and residents, was 7 percent, with none of the third-year students believing it. Across all questions, the belief composite mean was 11.5 percent. And while half believing at least one myth seems concerning, the rating of each individual myth is relatively low. Here is the list:

MYTH	Layman	1st YR	2nd YR	3rd YR	Resident
Whites have larger brains than blacks	12	2	1	0	0
Whites have a better sense of hearing compared with blacks	10	3	7	0	0
Blacks' nerve endings are less sensitive than whites'	20	8	14	0	4
Black people's blood coagulates more quickly than whites'	39	29	17	3	4
Whites have a more efficient respiratory system than blacks	16	8	3	2	4
Blacks have stronger immune systems than whites	14	21	15	3	4
Blacks have a more sensitive sense of smell than whites	20	10	18	3	7

Black couples are significantly more fertile than white couples	17	10	15	2	7
Blacks are better at detecting movement than whites	18	14	15	5	11
Blacks age more slowly than whites	23	21	28	12	14
Blacks' skin is thicker than whites'	58	40	42	22	25

Table 1[113]

This does not exactly portray an extreme level of belief in medical fallacies among medical students. It is not a good sign that medical students would think this, having achieved some level of training. However, since they were laymen prior to attending medical school, it can be said that as their learning increased, their belief in myths decreased. It would seem better for the surveyed pool of medical professionals to consist of actual doctors and medical school professors. Conducting the study with professors could also determine if these beliefs are being taught to medical students, an important step in suppressing medical myths.

---

[113] Kelly M. Hoffman, Sophie Trawalter, Jordan R. Axt, and M. Norman Oliver, "Racial bias in pain assessment and treatment recommendation, and false beliefs about biological differences between blacks and whites," *Proceedings of the National Academy of Sciences*, April 19, 2016. https://www.pnas.org/content/113/16/4296#sec-2

Villarosa ends with the argument that internalized racism and both conscious and unconscious biases drive doctors to go against their oath to do no harm. This may be true in the cases where racism is the cause of mistreatment, but she has not proven that is the case. Additionally, she argues that the effects of slavery create inequities today and cause many to blame individuals and their communities for statistically poor health outcomes. She suggests understanding that race is a proxy for bias, disadvantage, and ill-treatment would serve better than predicting disease or disability based on race. Perhaps awareness of both may be beneficial, but absolving a community or an individual of the responsibility of maintaining healthy habits is patronizing and dangerous.

18

American Popular Music

For centuries, black music, forged in bondage, has been the sound of complete artistic freedom. No wonder everybody is always stealing it.
—Wesley Morris

The quotation at the beginning of this essay, "Why Is Everyone Always Stealing Black Music?" is misleading. The author, film critic, and podcast host, Wesley Morris does not actually define what popular white artists have done as stealing. In fact, he describes his "conflation of pride and chagrin" anytime he hears a white person inhabiting blackness with gusto. He, like many other blacks, is half impressed by the ability of whites either to replicate the soul of the music or to successfully make it their own, and half offended by the song's success—as if it is somehow not authentic, or worse, taking opportunities away from a black artist. Either way, we sway to the music while scrutinizing the artist. Morris understands the complexities, but cannot resist the urge to call what he hears "blackness," even when performed by whites.

He recognizes, however, that American music has long been a complex mix. Genres and music segregated, yet the music is always a blend. It was inevitable. The excitement of hearing a new sound or a catchy tune sticks in your head; escaping it is impossible. It is like putting a bullet back into the barrel. And once it is in the ether, it cannot remain confined to segregated ears. The influence is circular. Morris describes a different sound in black music. A rougher, more syncopated sound, in contrast to the composed music of whites. Where this is true, it is based on influences rather than a genetic musical gene.

It is common for blacks to point out, as Morris has, the many popular artists who were greatly influenced by black artists. Some give credit; others do not. These examples are true, but rarely do we talk about the full kaleidoscope that has built and strengthened American popular music. Rap music was the sound of the streets of urban America, while heavy metal and hard rock were the voice of the frustrated white male, completely segregated. Then Rick Rubin and Russell Simmons fused the two on several tracks by LL Cool J, Run DMC, and the Beastie Boys. Soon, Public Enemy was sampling rock music on tracks, and Anthrax was rapping. There are many examples of this.

Most would agree that Rock and Roll is the original fusion point. Many think of it as just the Blues with an edge, but it was really a combination of Blues and Country, one black, the other white. Most of the popular music post–1960 can be traced back to it, and Chuck Berry is the undisputed king. What many do not know is that his sound was born from a fusion of country music. As Berry said in his book, *Chuck Berry: The Autobiography*,

"Curiosity provoked me to lay a lot of our country stuff on our predominantly black audience and some of our black audience began whispering 'Who is that black hillbilly at the Cosmo?'" If you're unsure of the fusion, check out Arthur Smith's 1948 track, *Guitar Boogie*,[114] recorded several years before Berry began performing.

Another example is Marvin Gaye, arguably the greatest Rhythm and Blues artist of all times. In David Ritz's biography, *Divided Soul*, Gaye was asked about his influences. He said, "My dream was to become Frank Sinatra. I loved his phrasing, especially when he was very young and pure.... He was the heavyweight champ, the absolute."[115] Later he would say about the producers at Motown pushing him to do Rhythm and Blues,[116] "The plan was to avoid shaking my ass on stage.... My model was Perry Como."

The point here is musical influences flow in every direction. It is beautiful, and it enriches us all. What Morris describes next is the opposite of this.

Morris makes his move to link slavery to today's American popular music. He tells the story of Thomas Dartmouth Rice, an obscure New York performer who changed entertainment in America for decades and created the seminal racist caricature used to further denigrate and mock Africans already tortured and subjugated by slavery. The beginning was innocuous. Here is how it is described:

---

114 Arthur Smith, "Guitar Boogie," performance archived at: https://www.youtube.com/watch?v=pksPotxh-vg

115 David Ritz, *Divided Soul: The Life of Marvin Gaye* (New York: De Capo Press, 1991), 29.

116 Compendium of Marvin Gaye R&B recordings at: https://www.discogs.com/Marvin-Gaye-The-Master-1961-1984/release/2070442

> He saw a decrepit, possibly disfigured old black man singing while grooming a horse on the property of a white man whose last name was Crow. On went the light bulb. Rice took in the tune and the movements but failed, it seems, to take down the old man's name. So, in his song based on the horse groomer, he renamed him: "Weel about and turn about jus so/Ebery time I weel about, I jump Jim Crow." And just like that, Rice had invented the fellow who would become the mascot for two centuries of legalized racism.

This was the beginning of Minstrel shows, and as they gained popularity, the acts increased. P.T. Barnum added minstrels to his "Greatest Show on Earth," and when he was short on acts, he would "black up" himself. Once, he needed a last-minute replacement, so he found a black kid he was told was a great performer, but the minstrel audience would not accept a real black performer. So he "greased the little nigger's face and rubbed it over with a new blacking of burned cork, painted his thick lips vermilion, put on a wooly wig over his tight curled locks and brought him out as 'the champion nigger-dancer of the world.'" This led to black minstrel performers.

Morris argues this led to a conundrum among black performers. To be acceptable to white audiences, black performers had to exude a near-perfect, clean-cut image. Inevitably, black audiences began to question the blackness of some artists. This questioning of blackness has come full circle. Morris questions if Flavor Flav and Kanye West's blackness is an act or if they are under white control. As an example, he uses a quote from an affluent black Republican lamenting that West's support of Trump is a "bad and embarrassing minstrel show served to only drive black people away from the GOP." It is interesting that he used this example when most of the attacks came from the left, and Don Lemon made a similar attack live on air at CNN.[117]

Morris points to Motown as the perfect mix of everything right about music, powered and packaged by blacks. They had the grit, soul, and improvisation that he earlier described as black music, the acceptability of Nat King Cole, the writing and arranging skills of classical musicians, and talent beyond comprehension. This changed the world. Black artists had perfected their sound, and they no longer would have to market their music for white audiences with ambiguous album covers. They would forever make their music, raw and real, and everyone would embrace it in its purest form.

This, Morris celebrates, constitutes a magnificent joke on American racism. But he points out that loving black music never meant loving black music. He ends with the story of "Old Town Road." Atlanta rapper Lil Nas X penned a simple song about a cowboy fantasy and posted it on social media. The song went viral and charted on the R&B and Country charts. Billboard removed the song from the charts, saying it did not have enough Country elements to it. The song was eventually remixed with Billy Ray Cyrus and went to number one on the Country charts.

This essay was not inflammatory like many of the others. It celebrated the struggle and triumph of black musicians without denigrating others. It was unnecessarily one-sided, but that is the

---

[117] Don Lemon, "Kanye West meeting with Trump a 'minstrel show,'" CNN broadcast, October 12, 2018, archived online at: https://www.youtube.com/watch?v=K-sNjEy6CCE

point of the Project. I will give Morris credit for at least having positive things to say about the black artists and even some of the white artists. For clarity's sake, Country radio did not refuse to play "Old Town Road"; Billboard just removed it from its charts. Aside from that, the only issue I have with the essay is that it does not connect today's music to slavery or the racist minstrel shows he described. Earlier, he said what was missing when whites did soul music was "centuries of weight." Well, that is missing in the music of the black artists as well.

19

Sugar

The sugar that saturates the American diet has a barbaric history as the 'white gold' that fueled slavery.
—Khalil Gibran Muhammad

The first thing we learn is that sugar is bad. It causes diabetes, obesity, and cancer. Americans consume twice the daily recommended amount per person, per year. Sugar is killing us all, and it is killing black people faster. This, of course, is not the point of the essay. The point is that the American sugar industry is as powerful as it is due to corporate welfare, in the form of subsidies and protectionist trade policies—and the brutality of slavery.

This essay, "The Barbaric History of Sugar in America," by Khalil Gibran Muhammad, professor at Harvard Kennedy School and the Radcliffe Institute, chronicles the history of sugar in America. How it began with Christopher Columbus bringing sugarcane from the Canary Islands. The sweetener had been discovered centuries before, but was a rare luxury because manufacturing it in bulk was so labor-intensive that no one would do the work—that is, without being forced. As Muhammad posits, "It seems reasonable to imagine that it might have remained so if it weren't for the establishment of an enormous market in enslaved laborers who had no way to opt out of the treacherous work." He is likely correct, at least for several decades.

Once the planters were able to process the sugar locally, plantations exploded along the Mississippi River. Muhammad describes the massive amounts of wealth this created for the sugar producers. It made Louisiana the second richest state and a burgeoning banking center. With its growth came an increase in slave labor as well as the cruelties that came with it. In the essay on capitalism, we were introduced to the brutal labor of the cotton fields. In many ways, the sugar plantations made the cotton fields look like office work.

Unlike the sun-up-to-sun-down toil of the cotton fields, the sugar houses operated night and day. The mills operated like dangerous manufacturing plants with no safety measures. There was constant risk of injury or death. Because of the demands and risks, more slaves were needed. As Muhammad describes it, "New Orleans became the Walmart of people-selling." Slave children were also forced to work in the mills to maximize production.

Here is how historian Michael Tadman described it: "Inadequate net nutrition meant that slaves working on sugar plantations were, compared with other working-age slaves in the United States, far less able to resist the common and life-threatening diseases of dirt and poverty."

Muhammad adds, "Life expectancy was less like that on a cotton plantation and closer to that of a Jamaican cane field, where the most overworked and abused could drop dead after seven years."

It is important to point out, in the context of this Project, that the planters were largely French or Spanish, and the conditions slaves lived under in Jamaica were worse; yet we are supposed to ignore this and maintain that the cruelties of slavery were unique to America.

Tiya Miles interrupts the sugar narrative with the amazing story of "The Enslaved Pecan Pioneer." She tells the story of how the pecan became popular among white Southerners, and they tried to find a way to standardize the tree. The trees produced nuts that varied widely in size, shape, and flavor. This went on for decades until a planter sent cuttings from his tree to his neighbor, J.T. Roman, the owner of Oak Alley Plantation. Roman gave the sample to a slave named Antoine, who successfully created the first commercially viable pecan varietal. Here is the story of a slave accomplishing what others were unable to do, despite his lack of formal training and under brutal, inhumane conditions. Their stories are surprisingly common; unfortunately, The 1619 Project rarely highlights them.

Muhammad fast-forwards to today. Adding insult to injury, much of the truth about the dark side of the sugar industry has been forgotten or whitewashed. He visits Whitney Plantation Museum, the only sugar-slavery museum in the nation. He notes, ironically, how the museum sits just across the river from the German Coast uprising of 1811,[118] one of the largest slave revolts in U.S. history, also largely forgotten. The Whitney Museum

[118] Rhae Lynn Barnes, "America's largest slave revolt: The German coast uprising of 1911," *U.S. History Scene*, undated. https://ushistoryscene.com/article/german-coast-uprising/

tries to give its visitors a true history of the plantation, hotel concierges, and tour operators, yet warns their guests that the Whitney is misrepresenting the past—trying to hold onto romantic ideas of the past.

Muhammad gives two examples of how the cruel treatment of blacks continues today. The first is the case of Angola, the largest maximum-security prison by landmass in the nation. It sits on a former plantation, and incarcerated men harvest sugarcane at the prison named for the plantation that formerly resided there. The second is the limited black sugar farmers. In slavery, and in most cases during Reconstruction, black Louisianans were not allowed to own property. They spent many years sharecropping or farming out their labor and expertise, usually for unfair wages.

He recounts how sometimes black workers demanded better conditions and pay. In some cases, things improved, but in others, white landowners responded with violence. Muhammad tells of a labor insurgency in 1887 led by a national labor union. In response, "at least 30 black people—some estimate hundreds—were killed in their homes and on the streets of Thibodaux, LA." Mary Pugh, a local white planter's widow, rejoiced to her son, "I think this will settle the question of who is to rule, the nigger or the white man, for the next 50 years!"

The unfair treatment continued into the twentieth century. In 1942, black men were lured to seasonal sugar jobs with the promise of high wages, only to have expenses for transportation, lodging, and equipment removed from their pay, drastically reducing their wages. When the workers tried to leave, they were captured or shot at while trying to hitch rides. The Department of Justice indicted the sugar company for carrying out a conspiracy to commit slavery. The indictment was ultimately quashed. In the 1980s, a congressional investigation found that sugar companies tried to exploit seasonal West Indian workers with threats of being sent back.

Black sugarcane farmers are rare today, and those numbers are dwindling. Most of the black farmers lost their land amid decades of racist actions by government agencies, banks, and real estate developers. The remainder claim they are being squeezed out. A black farmer, Wenceslaus Provost Jr., claims that M.A. Patout & Son, the largest sugarcane mill company in Louisiana, breached a harvesting contract in an effort to deliberately sabotage his business. Provost is also suing the First Guaranty Bank for claims related to lending discrimination. Eddie Lewis III says his land lease was terminated without just cause. The new lessee argues that "the Lewis boy" is "a horrible farmer" and has offered to pay Lewis $50,000 for his crops.

Muhammad is making the argument that this greed and discrimination is simply the standard operating procedure of the sugar industry—an industry manufacturing a toxic product, built on slavery, and maintained on systemic racism and government welfare. This is evidence that sugar, and its entire industry, is bad for all and worse for black people.

20

Mass Incarceration

Slavery gave America a fear of black people and a taste for violent punishment. Both still define our criminal-justice system.
—Bryan Stevenson

"Why American Prisons Owe Their Cruelty to Slavery," was written by Bryan Stevenson, a lawyer and founder and executive director of the Equal Justice Initiative. His work to help those who are innocent or who cannot afford a proper defense is commendable, particularly what he has done for offenders under the age of eighteen. While I understand the circumstances of each case are unique, the fact that sixty-two children in Louisiana have been sentenced to life in prison without parole for non-homicide offenses seems like the textbook definition of cruel and unusual punishment. This seems like something that can be rectified, as evidenced by the Supreme Court decision banning the sentences.

What is open for debate here is the implication that mass incarceration and excessive punishment are legacies of slavery.

There is no debating the numbers. As Stevenson states, in the early 1970s, there were fewer than 300,000 people in U.S. prisons; today, there are more than 2.2 million, with an additional 4.5 million on probation or parole. There may be a problem here, but providing numbers out of context does nothing but advance a one-sided argument. He assumes the growth is because of mandatory sentencing and "three strikes" laws. As evidence, he gives examples of extreme sentences his clients have received. I would assume he is omitting pertinent information, as I find it unlikely that it is common for a person to be sentenced to life in prison without parole for stealing a bicycle alone, as he claims.

He also fails to mention both that the population of the country has grown by more than 50 percent since the early 1970s and that crime—specifically, violent crime—increased dramatically from the 1970s through the mid-nineties. Ironically, crime began to fall after the passage of the much-decried 1994 Crime Bill and has been falling steadily for the past decade. Reducing the prison population is fine if it is not done at the expense of public safety. Regardless of the right approach, it is a stretch to link any of this to slavery.

The essay then describes the very real and very brutal laws and actions surrounding the punishment of Africans during slavery. In fact, what he describes is not criminal punishment; it is torture. He recounts the convenient racism of Alabama's Supreme Court, which in 1861 decided that slaves were regarded as persons when accused of crimes, but were considered property, not persons, in every other sense. The Thirteenth Amendment ended slavery, so racist whites created Black Codes, which essentially criminalized being black.

They used these Black Codes to criminalize things like being a group of black people out after dark, and seeking employment without a note from a former enslaver. Once imprisoned, they were then "leased" to businesses and farms, where they labored under brutal conditions. In 1916, Anthony Crawford was lynched in South Carolina for being successful enough to refuse a low price for his cotton. In 1933, Elizabeth Lawrence was lynched near Birmingham for daring to chastise white children who were throwing rocks at her.

After establishing how unfair and violent these Black Codes were, Stevenson fast-forwards one hundred years, stating that these Black Codes were the precursors of the modern criminal justice system. For him, Nixon's war on drugs, the mandatory minimum sentences, the three-strikes laws, children tried as adults, and "broken windows" policing are all essentially the same as the Black Codes of the Reconstruction Era. Driving while black, sleeping while black, sitting in a coffee shop while black, Stevenson argues, is the new language of "non-crimes." He claims these are situations where blacks are mistreated or arrested when the actions would have been ignored had they been white. He has no way of knowing this and provided no examples. He then points out that black kids are suspended and expelled at rates that vastly exceed the punishment of white children for the same behavior.

This is the way the left makes an argument. He states a fact with limited information, then forms a conclusion that cannot be drawn from the information provided. In his school discipline argument, for example, one important point that should be considered is the racial makeup of public-school students. In most urban areas, public-school populations are majority-minority. In Chicago, for instance, 87 percent of public-school students are minority. In New York City, the number is greater than 80 percent. The point is that the sheer population would dictate that minority students would be overrepresented in suspension and expulsion cases.

Another example Stevenson points to of racial disparities in the criminal justice system is the fact that black defendants are twenty-two times more likely to receive the death penalty for crimes whose victims are white. Here again, logic would contend that there are plausible reasons for many of these, but it is hard to explain twenty-two times more likely. I believe this too should be addressed, but I do not believe the solution is not to sentence heinous criminals to death just because they are black. Perhaps where the true racial disparity lies is in the fact that black murderers whose victims are white are far more likely to be captured than those with black victims. Those are some black lives who *should* matter.

Things Stevenson describes like solitary confinement and criminalizing blacks are wrong, and addressing them is a good thing. But living in the past and rehashing slavery is not the way to improve the system. He, and the others at The 1619 Project, are so focused on slavery and its impact that they fail to see any other cause of the mass incarceration of blacks. They see discrepancies and instantly assume a sinister plot. Even when presented with explanatory numbers, their sight is limited.

Because of the work Stevenson does, he is prone to take the most egregious cases and try to find justice. His work is needed, but he needs to be reminded of a reality that is plaguing the black citizens he professed to care about. There is a crime problem that disproportionately affects black communities. He focused a lot on youth criminals in his essay, but not once did he mention the fact that victimization rates and offender rates for blacks age fourteen to seventeen increased nearly 150 percent prior to the 1994 Crime Bill. It is disingenuous to ignore the crime stats, as crime levels correlate with incarceration rates.

The examples Stevenson uses to describe the Black Codes highlight innocent people being terrorized by racists. The policies he claims are "essentially the same" are addressing people who have broken the law. One can argue that the punishment is too harsh; but pretending they are the same, or condoning bad behavior to reduce the number of blacks in jail, only serves to satisfy some racial scorecard at the expense of the blacks in the community where these criminals do their damage.

21

The Wealth Gap

A vast wealth gap, driven by segregation, redlining, evictions, and exclusion, separates black and white America.
—Trymaine Lee

Trymaine Lee is a Pulitzer Prize-winning journalist. I agree more with his commentary than I do with any other essay in The 1619 Project. This is largely because it is the only essay that does not tie its topic directly to slavery. In the essay, "How America's Vast Racial Wealth Gap Grew: By Plunder," Lee does say that today's racial wealth gap is perhaps the most glaring legacy of American slavery, but I will just assume he meant Reconstruction. That blacks lag significantly behind whites in every economic indicator is a fact no one disputes. I would argue that it is also universally understood that much of that discrepancy, especially in the wealth gap, is due to systemic racism. The question is whether or not that systemic racism still exists.

Lee points out that today, whites have seven times the wealth of black Americans on average. Although they represent nearly 13 percent of the population, blacks hold less than 3 percent of the nation's wealth. As he points out, it is worse on the margins. According to the Economic Policy Institute, 19 percent of black households have zero or negative net worth. Just 9 percent of white families are that poor.

For the first seventy-five years post-slavery, this was nearly entirely the fault of the government, either by racist laws and practices or by negligence—taking no action as racist whites robbed, killed, and terrorized blacks. To illustrate this, Lee opens his essay with the tragic story of Elmore Bolling.

Bolling was a black businessman who was killed in Lowndesboro, Alabama, in 1947 for the crime of being too successful. A group of white men confronted him on a section of road he had helped lay and shot him seven times. His family rushed from their store to find him lying dead in a ditch. He was said to have wealth worth nearly $500,000 in today's dollars. His wealth was summarily stolen by white creditors and people posing as creditors. Within two years, the family was living in poverty, having had their wealth stolen by whites, and fled the county in fear for their lives.

Seventy years later, the effects of Bolling's murder are still felt by his children and their children. "There was no inheritance, nothing for my father to pass down, because it was all taken away," says Josephine Bolling McCall, the only one of Bolling's children to get a college degree. Of the seven siblings, those with more education fared best; the men struggled most, primarily working as low-paid laborers. Of Elmore and Bertha Mae's twenty-five grandchildren, only six graduated from college; of those, two are McCall's children. The rest are unemployed or underemployed. They have never known anything like the prosperity of their grandparents.

These types of actions were far too common. Armed white people stormed prosperous majority-black Wilmington, North Carolina, in 1898 to murder dozens of black people, force 2,000 others off their property, and overthrow the city government. In the Red Summer of 1919, at least 240 black people were murdered across the country. And in 1921, in one of the bloodiest racial attacks in United States history, Greenwood, a prosperous black neighborhood in Tulsa, Oklahoma, was burned and looted. It is estimated that as many as 300 black people were murdered, and 10,000 were rendered homeless. Thirty-five square blocks were destroyed. No one was ever convicted in any of these acts of racist violence.

These were obvious acts of terrorism, but the government also played an active role in suppressing economic opportunities for blacks. According to Lee, it started with a promise of compensation. In January 1865, General William Sherman issued an order reallocating hundreds of thousands of acres of white-owned land along the coasts of Florida, Georgia, and South Carolina for settlement by black families in forty-acre plots. When Lincoln was assassinated, Vice President Andrew Johnson effectively rescinded Sherman's order by pardoning white plantation owners and returning to them the land on which 40,000 or so black families had settled.

Even attempts by the government to improve things failed. Congress established the Freedmen's Bureau to oversee the transition from slavery to freedom, and the Freedman's Savings Bank was formed to help four million formerly enslaved people gain financial freedom. More than 60,000 black people deposited over $1 million into the Freedman's Savings Bank, but its all-white trustees began issuing speculative loans to white investors and corporations, and when it failed in 1874, many black depositors lost much of their savings.

The Black Codes and Jim Crow laws were a direct result of Andrew Johnson's unconditional pardon of the former members of the Confederacy, which led to their elections to Congress and judgeships, turning the South back over to former slaveholders in just over a decade. The government then moved from enforcing laws that directly prohibited blacks to excluding them from newly formed benefits.

Lee states that in the 1930s, President Franklin Roosevelt's New Deal helped build a solid middle class through sweeping social programs, including Social Security and the minimum wage. Unfortunately, most blacks worked in occupations that were ineligible for these benefits. The establishment of the Home Owners' Loan Corporation in 1933 helped save the collapsing housing market but excluded black neighborhoods. They were deemed "hazardous" and colored in with red on maps, a practice that came to be known as "redlining." Blacks suffered the same fate with the G.I. Bill. It provided for assistance with mortgages, but the loans guaranteed by the program went to developers who would not sell to blacks.

The immoral and illegal treatment of blacks is well-documented and accurate. Where Lee and others in the progressive racism movement miss the mark is more nuanced here, but still important.

First, they place too much blame on single events. For instance, Lincoln's assassination clearly set the nation back, and Andrew Johnson was a feckless, racist president; however, Lincoln was trying to find a way to repair the union at the height of the war, so there is no indication he would have kept the Confederate states out of the union.

This takes us to the ever-popular "40 acres." It is most likely that, like Johnson, Lincoln would not have upheld General Sherman's special field order. Either way, without actual legislation to the fact, there is no way the Taney Court would have upheld it if the landowners sued. William A. ("Sandy") Darity Jr., public policy professor at Duke University and the leading intellectual proponent for slavery reparations, states, "The origins of the racial wealth gap start with the failure to provide the formerly enslaved with the land grants of 40 acres."

He is right about the origin of the problem being with the government, but he is wrong about the specifics. I want to clearly state that I believe reparations were the correct response to slavery; I just believe the clock has run out on the payment. Those who were enslaved, and to an extent their children of a certain age, were due the payments. Making payments beyond that would be like me showing up at your door saying that you owe me the one hundred dollars your father, who has been dead for twenty years, took from me in 1990. Darity, and the proponents of reparations, are wrong in both the moral solution as well as its practicality.

If reparations had been given during Reconstruction, not only would the payments have gone to the people who had been wronged, but the payments would be coming from those personally responsible and others who were complicit. Payments made today would be funded by generations of people who had nothing to do with the atrocities, including some blacks. Next, there is the untold amount of wealth that was taken by racially motivated attacks like the Red Summer of 1919, Rosewood,

Tulsa, Wilmington, and others. No one was arrested in these incidents, so there is no way to get just compensation for them.

There may be a case for those omitted from federal programs designed to create a middle class and help people build wealth; but again, only those still living would qualify. I have no problem with evaluating and paying those who were wronged by these exclusions or affected directly by Jim Crow laws. However, those who compare slavery reparations to payments made to Japanese-Americans or Jews should be looking to Jim Crow or New Deal grievances as their comparison rather than slavery.

In any event, I think the reparations talk is short-sighted. Setting slavery aside, we are 155 years removed from slavery, and there is too much focus on the first one hundred years—and in the case of The 1619 Project, the first 345 years—and not enough on the last fifty-five years. Members of the progressive racism movement are, by definition, glass-half-empty types; all they see are the negatives.

Here is an example. Lee highlights the horrendous and inhumane actions of racist whites, but never stops to think that in order for whites to steal the wealth of blacks, blacks had to first amass wealth. Blacks earned their wealth with violent racists in their midst, laws passed specifically to make things difficult for them, and segregation. If blacks could produce at that level in the direst of circumstances and learn, build, create, and thrive, what is holding us back today? We have made great strides, but this focus on the past is stifling our progress. Blacks had more wealth and more successful businesses, in black neighborhoods, in the early twentieth century than we do now.

Some of that has to do with the end of segregation, allowing blacks more mobility and spreading that success to more areas. But in many ways, we are limiting ourselves. We still look at the government as an organization run by racist whites, but ignore the true change in front of us. Many people looked at the election of Barack Obama as a pivotal moment in the country's racial progress; but they ignore the fact that in the South—a part of the country still viewed as clinging to the past and romanticizing slavery—blacks have been winning elections for decades. Most of the blacks in Congress represent Southern states. Keep in mind, both Florida and Georgia had black politicians get 49 percent of the vote in statewide elections.

Additionally, how many know that Atlanta, Little Rock, Birmingham, Charlotte, and Jackson, Mississippi all have black mayors? Over one-third of blacks have college degrees. What are these elected officials and educated blacks doing to foster growth within the black community? More can be done, and the wealth gap needs to be addressed. But thinking slavery is the cause for current struggles, while knowing our unlimited opportunities, is an affront to our abilities and a slap in the face to our ancestors who worked so hard despite the obstacles they faced.

22

Why Can't We Teach This?

"We are committing educational malpractice": Why slavery is mistaught—and worse—in American schools.
—Nikita Stewart

In the final essay of the project, Nikita Stewart, an assistant editor at *The New York Times*, asks, "Why Can't We Teach This?" She opens with an overtly racist lesson from a book published in 1863. She admits that textbooks no longer publish overt lies, but the country still struggles to teach children about slavery. She argues that because states are not required to meet academic content standards, there is no consensus on the curriculum around slavery.

This is the problem with the entire premise of the essay, and I will address this and other problems as I answer the question posed in her title, "Why Can't We Teach This?"

Stewart is arguing for a uniform curriculum on slavery; I challenge the need for a slavery curriculum at all. Certainly, slavery should be taught in the context of history, and should not be sugar-coated. What she and the proponents of this Project want, though, is an educational curriculum that is centered on slavery. This would be an inaccurate and ineffective way to teach history. It would be like having a history course on boats. For centuries, navigational dominance was the number-one determinant of how strong a country or empire was and if it would develop faster than others. However, as important as this was to historical events, it is not a history course.

Before I go on, I must clarify, as I know some emotionally weak person will say that I am comparing slaves to a boat. That argument would be a clear indication of someone who should have no input in teaching our children. What I'm saying is that to the slaveowner, their "property" is important, and to the enslaved person, their freedom is everything. However, slavery was ubiquitous so, to the average person of the time, it was not a prevailing issue. At least not for hundreds of years. When it becomes a point of contention, then it is a topic to discuss. In discussing history from roughly 800 to 1700, it would rarely be more than a side note.

Back to Stewart's "slavery curriculum." She gleefully ponders what it would be like to properly teach students about enslavement. I contend that they do not really want to teach slavery honestly. If they did, they would not constantly refer to it as "American slavery." A true slavery course would teach about its origin, everywhere in the world it existed, where the 97 percent of slaves stolen from Africa ended up, and where slavery still exists today. They have no interest in teaching this class.

She also laments the fact that some teachers want to tell students about the "good" people, like the abolitionists and the black people who escaped to freedom, but leave out the details of why they were protesting or what they were fleeing. I will agree that this is a whitewashed version of history. But the violent, detailed examples of brutal slavery with no mention of the abolitionists is also a skewed version of history. Unless they are contending that there were no "good" white people in America between 1620 and 1964.

Stewart then uses research from the Southern Poverty Law Center, a biased, racist organization, to explain how biased and racist twelve textbooks used in high schools are. The Southern Poverty Law Center gave most textbooks an average grade of 46 percent. This is low, but much higher than the 11 percent reading proficiency and 12 percent math proficiency that Baltimore high school graduates rated.[119] Schools are failing students, mostly black, all over the country, but hey, if Stewart and her colleagues have their way, those students will know about the sugar mills.

Southern Poverty Law Center's director of Teaching Tolerance, Maureen Costello, tells Stewart, "The best textbooks maybe have 20 pages [about slavery], and that's in an 800-page textbook." What does that mean exactly? In the absence of a full course on slavery, how many pages in the book *should* be devoted to slavery? To highlight the problem with this, Stewart states that about 92 percent of students did not know that slavery was the war's central cause, according to the survey. This is only evidence

[119] Armstrong Williams, "Baltimore's failing schools are a tragedy of criminal proportions," *The Hill*, September 13, 2017. https://thehill.com/opinion/education/350315-baltimores-failing-schools-are-a-tragedy-of-criminal-proportions

of poor teaching. I am quite sure this could have been packed into the twenty pages on slavery.

Next, she asks, "How have we been able to fail students for so long?" In answer to her own question, she mentions *The Lost Cause*, a book by Edward A. Pollard that white southerners used to soften the brutality of enslavement. She neglects to mention that the book was written in 1866 and was largely out of use by the 1920s. In fact, David Saville Muzzey's *An American History*, published in 1911 to destroy the Lost Cause narrative, was the prevailing tool used to teach children American history for nearly fifty years.[120] However, using flawed books is only one of the failures she complains about; the other is all the white teachers. She writes:

> About 80 percent of this country's 3.7 million teachers are white, and white educators, some of whom grew up learning that the Civil War was about states' rights, generally have a hand in the selection of textbooks, which can vary from state to state and from school district to school district. "These decisions are being made by people who learned about slavery in a different way at a different time," Costello told me.

This invites a never-ending series of questions. What percentage of the teachers grew up learning the Civil War was about states' rights? How does she know how they learned about

---

[120] Connor King, "Lost cause textbooks: Civil War education in the South from the 1890s to the 1920s," Thesis, University of Mississippi, 2018, p. 39.

slavery, or if they had a hand in selecting textbooks? The more important question, however, is why are 80 percent of all teachers white? If black children learn better with black teachers and this topic is better taught by blacks, it seems that black adults have failed black children. There is a solution: recruitment. Is The 1619 Project going to shift its focus from slavery to recruiting black teachers?

Stewart says that teachers fail younger students by not teaching them that many of the nation's Founders owned slaves. She quotes another Southern Poverty Law Center comrade, Hasan Kwame Jeffries, who is an "expert" on teaching slavery. He recounts a story of his eight-year-old daughter's assignment that listed "fun facts" about George Washington. The assignment said he owned rabbits, to which Jeffries added, "He owned people, too." The assignment continued by saying that Washington lost his teeth and had to have dentures. Jeffries added, "Yes, he had teeth made of slaves." This from the chair of the Southern Poverty Law Center's Teaching Hard History advisory board.

Challenging The 1619 Project's approach to teaching slavery does not mean they are wrong about everything. Some of the American history taught in schools has been whitewashed. Thomas Jefferson's relationship with Sally Hemings was described as "intimacy" and an "affair" in a textbook, descriptions the Southern Poverty Law Center find problematic. A quote from the textbook states, "White masters all too frequently would force their attentions on female slaves, fathering a sizable mulatto population, most of which remained enchained." They claim that is a delicate way to describe rape, but one wonders how descriptive do they want it? It does say "force" and "enchained." This example is hardly misinformation.

Adding more context to the discussion of slavery is fine, but going into graphic descriptive detail provides little education. To the point of educational value, proponents of the Project never say what the benefits of creating a full curriculum surrounding slavery would be. From a practical standpoint, the school day will not be extended, so there will not be time for additional coursework. Something will have to be removed to make room for this new slavery focus. Many of our schools have been without a robust civics education for years, and lately, they have had their music programs cut. What will slavery replace?

Stewart asks, "Why can't we teach this?" Here is the answer to her question. The 1619 Project cannot be taught because it is a toxic, anti-American, politically biased, defeatist collection of propaganda. While it is wrapped in enough truth to prevent it from being classified as fiction, its core is opinion and should not be allowed anywhere near a social studies or history classroom. Its greatest tool is lies of omission.

The revisionist history starts with the Project's name. The year 1619 is when the first slaves arrived in America; therefore, they insist, that is when the country started—a point they now claim was always intended to be a work of "memory," not history. That memory is flawed. Even if you give them their argument and accept that the Plymouth Rock story was an example of "whitewashing" our beginning, and that the true beginning of America was in 1619 Jamestown, this does not start the slavery story in "America."

As Olivia Waxman, staff writer for *Time History*, notes, "Nor is it the case that those who arrived in 1619 were the first enslaved people in what would become the United States. In 1565, for example, the Spanish brought enslaved Africans to present-day St. Augustine, Fla., the first European settlement in what's now the continental U.S."[121] And this is just the European enslavement. If the behaviors of man across time are consistent in the Americas, as it was everywhere else, it would be logical to assume some Native American tribes enslaved members of other tribes. None of this is consistent with their "slavery is uniquely an American institution" rhetoric, so it is ignored.

I understand the point is to rectify the whitewashing of the violent debasement of blacks during slavery. However, their overcorrection is shocking. They go through graphic detail highlighting many examples in each essay. Worse, they describe whites as a monolith. The country was founded on slavery, anti-black racism is in its DNA, and these problems persist today These are the Project's core beliefs, and there is no room for nuance.

There is no talk of evangelicals starting the abolitionist movement, John Brown's Harper's Ferry raid, or the fact that twenty of the thirty-five states had already abolished slavery before the Civil War. The Founders are only described as racist slaveowners who did not believe blacks deserved rights. In the interest of accurate education, there should be some mention of the Founders' writings against slavery. There were many, yet not one quote is listed in the entire Project. They also do not mention that several Founders did not own slaves, only that ten of the first twelve presidents were slaveowners.

It is also politically biased, although they try not to make it obvious. They could not describe Reconstruction without placing Democrats and Republicans on the proper side; however, they

121 Olivia B. Waxman, "The first Africans in Virginia landed in 1619. It was a turning point for slavery in American history—but not the beginning," *TIME*, August 20, 2019. https://time.com/5653369/august-1619-jamestown-history/

subtly try to frame the parties in today's context. They never mention the Radical Republicans and describe them as "left" and their actions as "egalitarian." They also hint at the alleged party shift, trying to imply that those racists are now Republicans. In the essay on democracy, Republicans are called extremists, nullifiers, and insurgents for their actions under President Obama, but the same actions by Democrats under President Trump were not mentioned.

They unartfully and illogically link every issue in the Project not to racism, but to slavery. Slavery alone made America rich, slavery is stopping us from having universal healthcare, slavery is the reason people defend states' rights (even though it is clearly listed in the Constitution), slavery is the reason blacks have diabetes, and finally, slavery is the reason whites enjoy soul music.

With all its focus on blacks, you would think there would be as many examples of black hope and triumph as there are of black subjugation. This is not the case. If they are not going to give an even-handed account of whites in America, the least they could do is offset the putrid hatred of slavery with examples of those who overcame it. This is rarely done, and when it is, the positives are quickly taken away by those whites with the bad DNA. There is no mention of the great strides we have made as a country and as a people. Instead, all that time is spent on what was taken from blacks and the struggles they face today. That struggle seems magnified because black progress is measured against whites, rather than viewed relative to where blacks used to be.

Finally, conceding that there is room for growth in the black community, there are no solutions suggested by the Project and nothing positive to take away. There is a brief mention of reparations but nothing about opportunities or personal empowerment. Since every problem has been caused by slavery, why would they suggest blacks do anything to improve their own lives? Even where they call for government redress, they ignore the tremendous political power blacks wield today. Most of the largest cities in the country have black elected officials who are empowered to make the necessary changes they seek. The South, which is viewed with disdain by the essayists, boasts more black elected officials than any other part of the country.

The 1619 Project cannot and should not be taught because it will be detrimental to all Americans, especially black Americans. It would take valuable classroom time away from STEM or improving already low reading and math proficiency levels, in order to create a generation of angry, entitled youth with a skewed view of America, the greatest nation on God's green earth.

23

Time to Act

Progressive racism is dangerous for our society and it is outrageous that so many people are being swept up by it. It is immoral, unconstitutional, and regardless of how it is framed, furthers inequality. Has anyone stopped to ask who gets to decide when racism is justified and when it is bad? Once you convince people it is okay, how far will it go? When does it end? Only time will tell but the progressive racists are just getting started.

First, we had The 1619 Project quietly infiltrating our public schools. In September 2019, one month after its publication, Janice Jackson, CEO of the Chicago Public Schools, announced that The 1619 Project would be part of the school system's curriculum.[122] Before parents could be made aware of the toxic and

[122] Janice K. Jackson, "The 1619 Project and Chicago Public Schools," Chicago Public Schools, September 17, 2019. https://blog.cps.edu/2019/09/17/the-1619-project-and-chicago-public-schools/

misleading content of the Project, it had already spread to 4,500 schools across the country.[123]

Next, were the open attacks on whites. Ibram X. Kendi, author of *How to Be an Antiracist*, claims that lack of racist intent is not enough, whites must be "anti-racists," actively fighting racial disparities or the racist actions of others, or they are also racist. Robin DiAngelo takes this a step further in her book, *White Fragility*, claiming that all whites are racist and those who do not admit it are simply fragile due to an oversized sense of superiority.

And now the talk has shifted to critical race theory. These are all variations of the same argument. The systems and institutions that undergird America are tainted, to their core, by racism. We must view everything through a prism of race to inoculate the country against its racist infection. The acceptance of this culminated with President Biden signing dozens of executive orders and stating that promoting "racial equity" is an issue of the whole of government.[124] Anyone could have predicted the reaction to this cultural shift.

Aggressive radicals, propped up by the president, are now demanding immediate change. It started with a focus on creating a façade of racial equity. To accomplish this, people needed to see more minorities in positions of power. A move started to

---

[123] Hannah Farrow, "The 1619 Project curriculum taught in over 4,500 schools — Frederick County Public Schools has the option," Medill News Service, July 21, 2020. https://dc.medill.northwestern.edu/blog/2020/07/21/the-1619-project-curriculum-taught-in-over-4500-schools-frederick-county-public-schools-has-the-option/#sthash.5XJnxg7P.dpbs

[124] "Biden says promoting racial equity is an issue of 'the whole of government,'" Yahoo News, January 26, 2021. https://news.yahoo.com/biden-says-promoting-racial-equity-202405213.html

replace some white and male leaders with blacks and women. The CEO of Citigroup stepped down and was replaced with a woman[125]; the white police chief in Portland stepped down and requested they replace her with a black man[126]; the *Bachelor* host, Chris Harrison was replaced by a black man[127]; and President Biden bragged he will have, "the most diverse Cabinet anyone in American history has ever announced."[128]

Unfortunately, they quickly realize that equality, or equity as they now frame it, will not come from a handful of minorities getting new positions. They decided the best way to effect change is to make race a determining factor in as many areas as possible—the textbook definition of racism. To do this, they trample on the very law most Americans, especially liberals, celebrate as a seminal shift in greater equality for the country, The Civil Rights Act of 1964.

Equality is not the goal for this new group of progressives. They will stop at nothing short of equity. They now want race

---

125 Martin Baccardax, "Citigroup: Jane Fraser becomes first woman to lead a U.S. megabank following retirement of Michael Corbat," *The Street*, September 10, 2020. https://www.thestreet.com/investing/citigroup-ceo-michael-corbat-retires-replaced-by-jane-fraser

126 "Portland's Police Chief steps down so black officer could take her place," *Bet*, June 10, 2020. https://www.bet.com/news/national/2020/06/10/portland-police-chief-resigns-george-floyd-protest.html

127 Alaa Elassar, "Emmanuel Acho will host 'The Bachelor: After the Final Rose Special,' replacing Chris Harrison," *CNN*, February 28, 2021. https://edition.cnn.com/2021/02/27/entertainment/emmanuel-acho-the-bachelor-host-chris-harrison-trnd/index.html

128 Julia Manchester, "Biden defends Cabinet choices after criticism: 'Most diverse Cabinet' in history," *MSN News*, December 4, 2020. https://www.msn.com/en-us/news/politics/biden-defends-cabinet-choices-after-criticism-most-diverse-cabinet-in-history/ar-BB1bCfOn

to be the determining factor in many decisions including school admissions,[129] government assistance,[130] medical care,[131] and commercial pilots.[132] They will soon find that, like the aesthetic attempt to create a racial utopia, this cannot create the racial equity they are hoping for. It is destined to fail due to what I call the guacamole problem.

Let us say there is a perceived issue of guacamole inequality and the government is going to fix it. They mandate that every government body has a designated amount of guacamole. They then force businesses and individuals, of a certain income, to purchase a certain amount of guacamole. Somehow, guacamole inequality still exists. They realize that they spent so much time focused on guacamole that they never ensured there were enough avocados to meet the new demand. This is what they are trying with the black community, forcing "opportunities" for blacks while doing nothing to prepare them for these created opportunities. If they don't grow and cultivate the avocadoes, they will never achieve guacamole equality.

---

[129] Eliza Shapiro, "New York City will change many selective schools to address segregation," *The New York Times*, December 18, 2020. https://www.nytimes.com/2020/12/18/nyregion/nyc-schools-admissions-segregation.html

[130] The Oregon Cares Fund website: https://www.theoregoncaresfund.org/

[131] Sam Dorman, "NYC chief medical officer calls for racial preferences in medical care, criticizes 'colorblind' practices," *Fox News*, March 29, 2021. https://www.foxnews.com/us/nyc-doctor-racial-preference-minorities-medical-care

[132] Karen Townsend, "More airline wokeism: United Airlines' new diversity goals for pilot trainees sets quotas," *Hot Air*, April 8, 2021. https://hotair.com/karen-townsend/2021/04/08/more-airline-wokeism-united-airlines-new-diversity-goals-for-pilot-trainees-sets-quotas-n381933

Those interested in making a more perfect union, should be fully committed to equality. Understanding that some people will not achieve the same level of success, efforts can then be made to help those in need. Instead, the progressive racists choose to tear down the country by conflating the flaws of individuals with the "system." What is most appalling is they ignore the great things about the country, many of them unique in the world, in order to focus on what they see as irredeemable characteristics, most based on false premises.

Black Lives Matter is based on the argument that police are regularly executing black men, many of them unarmed. For this to be true, one must believe that the police are willing to shoot innocent blacks but prefer to arrest guilty ones. What other explanation could there be for intelligent people to argue both that black men are being hunted down and killed by police *and* that mass incarceration of blacks is a problem? How do so many black men end up in jail without being shot?

The 1619 Project is based on the belief that America was founded on slavery and could not have happened without it. To make their case, they point to the Jamestown colonists who arrived with twenty to thirty slaves. Though they are incorrect about America's founding, this is not the false premise to which I am alluding. The argument they make is that the wretched institution of slavery is somehow unique to America. However, no one disputes the fact that slavery existed in Europe at the time. So, why would Europeans need to leave Europe to practice slavery? The argument lacks logical thought.

The progressive racism movement is anti-American. Black Lives Matter makes demands—end prisons, remove borders, eliminate capitalism—that, if enacted, would end the country as we know it. The 1619 Project claims that all our problems are due to slavery and anti-black racism, and these beliefs are in our DNA. They also profess that American capitalism is bad and our founding principles are a lie. No honest person can believe any of this about the country and still profess to support it.

The movement is destructive. Black Lives Matter openly calls for a by-any-means-necessary approach to enacting its agenda. This includes threats and blackmail. They claim the system is racist, yet they are pushing for laws based on race. Their demands will lead to a weaker country and more devastation in the black community. The 1619 Project is indoctrinating kids through deliberate negative imagery, without context. The Project is wholly negative, with no solutions proffered. Actively teaching children a limited history of blacks and whites can only lead to a generation of angry blacks and depressed whites.

While the movement is bad for all Americans, it is especially detrimental to black Americans. If they were empowering them or giving them steps to improve their lives, there could be some merit to the movement, but they do not even feign a desire to do so. The essayists at The 1619 Project and the unnamed people who put together the platform for the Movement for Black Lives are educated and by all accounts successful. Why aren't they providing blacks with tips and tools to navigate this alleged racist system? Clearly, there is a formula that works, since they, and millions of other blacks, have done it.

Most importantly, they refuse to demand people take personal responsibility for their lives. Allowing people to abdicate their responsibilities and blame others is the entire idea behind this progressive racism movement. They argue that the bad things that happen to blacks in America are a result of systemic racism or slavery, never the result of poor actions on the part of the individual. Responsible parents would not raise their children this way, yet these groups advise millions of black people to surrender their lives to this counterproductive theory. They reduce all problems to a singular cause: white people.

For their part, whites are contributing to the problem. There are a few who push back, but most do not understand the damage being done, so they are unable or unwilling to offer any resistance. They are just fed up, understandably, with being called racist. But if they do not understand what these groups believe and what they want to achieve, they cannot be effective. And since most people will not speak up, you have a small number of people who can easily be labeled as "fringe." Members of the movement, and the complicit media, will simply say those vocal whites are examples of the racism they seek to stamp out.

What is worse are the white liberals who have given their complete support to this exclusionary movement. If everything is tied to slavery, as The 1619 Project suggests, then they are the modern-day embodiment of the John C. Calhoun wing of racism. I call them "compassionate supremacists." They openly state that blacks are worse off than whites and can never improve their lives without whites taking the lead. They support fewer police, but only in the black neighborhoods they rarely frequent. They agree that they have white privilege and verbally renounce it, but will not give up their power, jobs, or take a pay cut. It is all virtue-signaling, empty statements designed to make them feel better, not to help blacks.

Throughout the book, I have clearly highlighted the problem. Just as saying, "The system is racist" does not create opportunities, simply saying "They are wrong" will not slow the push to promote these racist ideas in schools or government agencies. It will also do nothing to help minimize the racial disparities in the areas of economics, criminal justice, and education.

There are several things we can do to push back against the race-focused ideologies that are taking hold of our culture.

We must first resist the urge to dismiss them. Too often, people hear a radical idea and assume everyone will understand that it is bad. The fact that schools are adopting The 1619 Project and corporations are giving millions to the Black Lives Matter movement shows that this is not the case. Part of the reason we have devolved to this point is that too many do not want to engage. I have had people ask me why I talk about race so often. I tell them that as long as it is dominating the conversation, someone must be willing to provide context and solutions. Remaining silent creates a situation where the extremists are the only ones being heard.

I believe challenging their rigid beliefs is the best way to show the flaws in their argument. Whenever you have the opportunity, you should question them on their ideas. Most people who support these ideas know the talking points but cannot draw a logical conclusion from them. The same goes for the people who started these movements. It is not for a lack of intelligence or critical thinking skills. These are not dumb people. They are well-educated and well-read. In some cases, they are experts in their area of study. I call them emotionally weak and intellectually lazy surface thinkers.

What this means is that, for some, it does not matter what the facts say; they are led by emotions. Others have a belief and will only use information that supports it. They are too lazy to search for alternative information, and when facts surface that contradict their beliefs, they ignore them. I point out that they are often highly educated because their education often exacerbates the problem. It increases the likelihood that people will take them at their word. It is the reason Linda Villarosa can write so eloquently about the horrors of medical experiments during slavery, then use that backdrop to imply those racist myths are still believed today. Her evidence is that less than fifteen medical students out of 222 believed that blacks have less sensitive nerve endings than whites.

The same goes for Bryan Stevenson. He is a successful attorney who fights to help inmates who were given excessive sentences and has argued in front of the Supreme Court. Why wouldn't we believe him? However, it does not seem honest or impartial to write an essay about mass incarceration and never mention crime. Isn't that why people are imprisoned? In his view of America, children are given life sentences for stealing bicycles, yet no one commits murder or rape. So, while these groups call for criminal justice reform and the abolition of police, no one asks them what will happen to the communities to which these criminals will return. This is a better reply than, "That's racist!"

The best course of action for those who want to invest in a long-term fix is to fight for our children. I often say that education should be the hill on which conservatives are willing to die. There is no more important topic. For decades, conservative Americans have ceded the educational system to the left. Now we are reaping what we have sown. We need to wrestle it back. Ideally, we would do everything we can to prevent The 1619 Project from being added to the school curricula, but this is likely too late. Many school districts have already decided to implement it. It is not too late to try to pressure them to reverse course, but we need to be ready with alternatives.

One great alternative is provided by my organization, Seeking Educational Excellence.[133] Founded to give struggling families

[133] Seeking Education Excellence website: https://1619exposed.com/

the tools to help their children succeed, the focus has always been to advance STEM and critical thinking skills rather than a social-justice narrative. With the advancement of progressive racism, Seeking Educational Excellence has launched an educational curriculum with a heavy focus on civics and history. We aim to provide an accurate depiction of American history, including its flaws, with context and without throwing out all that is great and unique about America. The curriculum will include materials that directly challenge and correct the information these groups offer as the truth about America.

For example, in the Project essay, "Undemocratic Democracy," there was a clear attack on states' rights. The point was to claim it was born out of slavery and is a "right-wing" issue today. This shows extreme ignorance on the author's part. Regardless of your views on states' rights, it is written into the Constitution, yet that is never mentioned in the essay. Second, and more important, states' rights is not a "right-wing" issue. It is the reason there were "free states" during slavery and the reason there are "sanctuary cities" today. The states' rights debate is an important one to have because it is one that few understand. An honest debate about it may provide much-needed education. It can start with better education.

Another alternative is 1776 Unites.[134] Founded by Bob Woodson, civil rights activist and Chairman of the Woodson Center, 1776 Unites represents a nonpartisan and intellectually diverse alliance of writers, thinkers, and activists focused on solutions to our country's greatest challenges in education, culture, and upward mobility. Where the progressives are highlighting racism and negativity, the approach of 1776 Unites is one of hope

134 1776 Unites website: https://1776unites.com/

and triumph. The organization recently launched a curriculum to add context to the one-sided message of The 1619 Project. This is how the curriculum is described on the site:

> The 1776 Unites curriculum offers authentic, inspiring stories from American history that show what is best in our national character and what our freedom makes possible even in the most difficult circumstances. 1776 Unites maintains a special focus on stories that celebrate black excellence, reject victimhood culture, and showcase African-Americans who have prospered by embracing America's founding ideals.[135]

Next, we need to weaken the support for The 1619 Project. This is the most difficult task, but we cannot let them drown out logic. Celebrities and billionaires with an anti-American, leftist agenda cannot be swayed, but we can address corporations. I do not mean boycotts; I mean clear, honest dialogue. Tens of thousands of people filling corporate social media accounts, emails, and phone lines, asking if they support bad behavior, can help. Ask them if they support the Civil Rights Act of 1964; all will undoubtedly say yes; then follow with, "If so, why are you willing to manage your business based on race?"

We must be vocal. Nearly everyone I know has had management mention Black Lives Matter or race at their job. This is not the time to ignore it. When my company sent out an email supporting "the movement," I immediately scheduled a meeting

---

135 The portal to the 1776 Unites curriculum is: https://1776unites.com/our-work/curriculum/

with the manager who sent it out and explained their platform and what it truly means for black people. He apologized and sent an email advising people to vet organizations before donating. The company is also not donating to them.

You may be thinking that you are white, so you do not have the leeway I do. You are right, and that is the problem. For too many years, blacks were treated as second-class citizens; however, the solution is not to assume we know better because we are black. Not only does it make no sense, but it is also impractical. What happens when two black people have opposing ideas; how do you determine who is right? Do we decide which of them is blacker?

There is a way in this climate for whites to push back against these racist ideas. The first step is to get educated. If you are going to engage, you will experience push-back, so you need to know your facts cold. Next, be like Columbo.

For those too young to remember, Columbo was a popular TV series starring Peter Falk. It centered around a homicide detective who was very shrewd, but whose speech and mannerisms gave the illusion of ineptitude, which often caused his suspects to drop their guard and make a mistake. This is the approach whites should take. Once comfortable with the information, do not challenge directly; just ask probing questions that will expose flaws or the ignorance of the presenter. In most cases, you never have to voice your disagreement with the idea or the movement.

Say, for example, you work at an accounting firm, and they are implementing a new focus on diversity. Management has decided to hire more black accountants. You would ask, "What is the unemployment rate for black accountants?" They will likely be confused. You then ask, "Where will we find the recruits?" The point is that there is virtually no unemployment among blacks with CPA designations. The same goes for engineers, doctors, and any other licensed professionals. Companies who take this approach will likely reshuffle people employed by other firms. Other than some healthy raises, nothing will change.

An approach I have seen someone else do that I loved was questioning the realities. So, you are on a call and the topic is diversity and inclusion. The presenter is talking about bias and how the company will be dedicated to improving its performance. A participant asks, "Can you give us some examples of what has been going on so we know what needs to change?" The presenter had none; she could only say that they wanted to make sure that BIPOC feel comfortable. These are just two of the many possible examples.

The most effective tool we have is our speech. We must share factual information. I tell everyone I know that it is important to work this into conversations with everyone they know. They should share it on social media, but it is also important to discuss it, adjusted for the relationship, with everyone they know in the real world. Family, friends, co-workers, Uber drivers, cashiers—they all count. Obviously, this does not mean deep conversations in the grocery line, but you can make a small comment based on the interaction. Ask a gig worker if they like what they do, then ask if it would be better for them to be an employee.

Finally, I ask that you promote this book and share it. Post quotations on social media and use it as a tool to teach the people you know who are not extremist, but simply do not understand what is at stake.

The one thing that gives me hope is the fact that most Americans do not agree with the progressive racists; we are just losing the messaging battle. I am surprised by how many people I talk to who have never heard of The 1619 Project. They all know Black Lives Matter but do not know how expansive the movement is, what they honestly believe, or what their endgame is. Educating the masses and exposing the lies of the progressive racism movement is our best hope at saving the country.

Acknowledgments

While this book is my effort to bring logic and context to the argument of race, which is being perpetuated by those demanding preference, it was not my idea to write it. For that I have David Bernstein from Emancipation Books to thank. It is a serious topic that needs to be addressed logically, and I am thankful that, with the many people writing on the subject, he allowed me a platform to use my unique voice to explain the myriad problems with the progressive racism movement, most notably Black Lives Matter and The 1619 Project.

It took a lot of work and many people to help me complete this book, but there are a few who deserve to be singled out for praise. I would like to thank Paul Beston and Nora Kenney from *City Journal*, Seth Barron from *The American Mind*, and David DesRosiers from *RealClearPolitics* for giving me a platform to write on these cultural issues; Professor Jason Hill, without whom David would not have known I existed; Dennis and Susan Prager, for their encouragement and tireless fighting to defend the values we hold dear.

I would also like to thank Kevin Jackson, for his advice and guidance as well as his leadership at Seeking Educational Excellence; and Bob Woodson, for the gargantuan effort to push back against The 1619 Project and to allow me on a team with unmatched intellectuals like Glenn Loury, Wilfred Reilly, Ian Rowe, John McWhorter, and so many more. It is an honor just being able to absorb the knowledge base 1776 Unites provides.

My thanks as well to Larry Schweikart and David Shestokas for giving me great insight when I have a historical or constitutional question and Chris Rufo for his relentless effort to fight the progressive racism movement. Thanks to the team at Emancipation Books who took my stew of ramblings, ideas, references, and rebuttals and made them the well-versed book you get to enjoy.

To my friends who challenge me to maintain a heightened level of critical thinking, I owe a sincere debt of gratitude. Here are some, but not all, who come to mind: Ari, Chavis, Bethany, Jeannie, Joanna, and Stephanie. Finally, to my family for sacrificing so that I can complete this—you are much of the reason this is so important.

Movement for Black Lives Proposed Legislation

- Antiterrorism and Effective Death Penalty Act (AEDPA)
- Black Maternal Health Momnibus Act of 2020
- CARE Act
- Deaths in Custody Reporting Act
- Dignity for Detained Migrants Act
- Disability Integration Act
- Dismantle Mass Incarceration for Public Health Act
- Domestic Violence Survivors Justice Act
- DREAM Act
- Electronic Communications Privacy Act (ECPA)
- EMPOWER Care Act
- End Corporal Punishment in Schools Act
- End Qualified Immunity Act
- End Racial and Religious Profiling Act of 2019
- Equality Act
- H.R.7143 (To repeal the military surplus program)
- Illegal Immigration Reform and Immigrant Responsibility Act
- Justice in Forensic Algorithms Act
- Medicare for All (2019) Act

- MERCY Act
- Mississippi Correctional Safety and Rehabilitation Act of 2020
- MORE Act
- National Domestic Workers' Bill of Rights
- New Way Forward Act
- NO BAN Act
- Paycheck Fairness Act
- PEACE (Police Exercising Absolute Care with Everyone) Act
- People's Justice Guarantee
- Prison Litigation Reform Act
- PUSHOUT! (Ending Punitive, Unfair, School-Based Harm that is Overt and Unresponsive to Trauma) Act
- REAL Act
- Repeal HIV Discrimination Act
- SAFE SEX Workers Study Act
- Schedules that Work Act
- Security and Financial Empowerment (SAFE) Act
- Stop Militarizing Law Enforcement Act
- Stop Shackling and Detaining Pregnant Women Act
- Therapeutic Fraud Prevention Act